NIKOLAOS A. VRISSIMTZIS

LOVE, SEX & MARRIAGE
IN ANCIENT GREECE

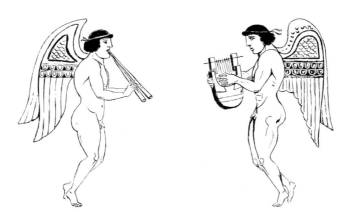

A guide to the private life of the ancient Greeks

To my mother
for a thousand reasons,
to Julian,
and to goddess Athena.

LOVE, SEX AND MARRIAGE
IN ANCIENT GREECE

Third Edition 1997

ISBN 960-90162-0-0

Copyright © 1995 by Nikolaos A. Vrissimtzis
P.O.Box 60102
15310 Agia Paraskevi
GREECE

Edited by	Wendy Hart
Drawings	Claude Rigouzzo
Map	Alexandros Krasokeras
Cover and Art direction	Leda Varvaroussi
Color separation	TOP COLOR
Production	POLYGRAMA

Front cover: Scene at a Symposion (detail). End of 6th c. B.C.
Royal Museums of Art and History – Brussels, R 351.

Printed in Greece.

CHRONOLOGICAL TABLE

B.C.

c.6000–3500	Neolithic period. Agriculture, stock-breeding, earliest pottery.
c.3500–2600	Sesklo civilization in mainland Greece, Cycladic civilization in the Aegean Sea.
c.2600–1600	Minoan civilization in Crete. Palaces of Knossos and Phaistos.
c.1600–1100	Mycenean civilization. Mycenae, Tiryns, Pylos. Trojan War.
c.1100– 750	First Greek colonies in Asia Minor. Geometric period.
776	First Olympic Games
750–490	Archaic period. Greek colonization of the coasts of the Mediterranean. Aristocratic rule replaced by tyrannies. Corinth and Aegina predominant sea powers. Solon's reforms. Tyranny of Peisistratos in Athens followed by Kleisthenes and democratic rule. Revolt of Greek city-states in Asia Minor against Persia.
490–479	Persian Wars: battles of Marathon and Thermopylae, sea-battles of Salamis and Mycale, battle of Plataea, and Persian final defeat and withdrawal.
479–458	Beginning of Athenian supremacy at sea. Kimon. Influence of Pericles begins.
458–446	Peace with Persia. Initial works at Parthenon.
446–431	Golden days of Pericles. Parthenon is completed. Beginning of the Peloponnesian War.
429	Plague in Athens and death of Pericles.
428–404	Athenian expedition against Sicily. Battle of Aegospotami, final defeat of Athens and submission to Spartan rule.
371–362	Rise of Thebes. Battle of Leuktra and Spartan defeat.
360–336	Philip II becomes king of Macedonia. Battle of Chaironeia and subjugation of the Greek cities to Philip. Assassination of Philip in 336. His son Alexander the Great succeeds to power.
334–323	Alexander the Great conquers Egypt, the Middle East and Asia as far as India. Death of Alexander in 323.
322–146	Succession wars. Pyrrhus rises to power in Epirus. Expedition against Italy. Decline of Greek kingdoms. Destruction of Corinth by the Romans and final subjugation of Greece.

ABOUT THE AUTHOR

Nikolaos A. Vrissimtzis was born and raised in Athens, Greece. He studied political sciences, sociology, history of art, and languages, in Athens and in Paris. He traveled a lot and published articles and photographs in most leading Greek magazines. He is the author of the books *"Greek Temples and Theaters,"* and *"Railroad Stations of Greece."* He lives and works in Athens.

ACKNOWLEDGMENTS

The author is grateful to all the museums and institutions which granted permission to reproduce photographs from exhibits in their collection. He also wishes to thank Mr. Claude Rigouzzo for his kind contribution of the "Eros" drawings.

BIBLIOGRAPHY

Calame, C.   *L' amore in Grecia.* Bari, 1983.
Dover, K.J.   *Greek Homosexuality.* London, 1978.
Flacelière, R.   *La vie quotidienne en Grèce au siècle de Périclès.* Paris, 1959. – *L'amour en Grèce.* Paris, 1971.
Fraser, L.C.   *Wedding Scenes on Attic Vases.* 1985.
Johns, C.   *Sex or Symbol?* London, 1978.
Keuls, E.C.   *The Reign of the Phallus.* 1985.
Licht, H.   *Sexual Life in Ancient Greece.* London, 1994.
Marcadé, J.   *Eros Kalos.* Genève.
Mossé, C.   *La femme dans la société Homérique.* Paris, 1981. – *La femme dans la société grecque ancienne.* Paris, 1983.
Reinsberg, C.   *Ehe, Hetärentum und Knabenliebe im antiken Griechenland.* München, 1989.

CONTENTS

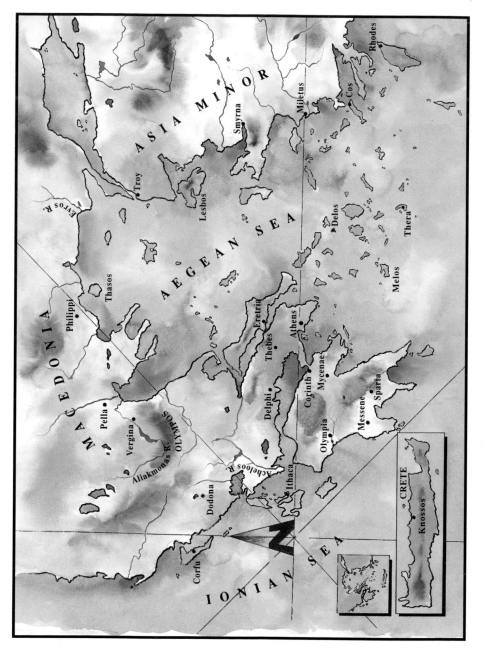

Greece in the times of Alexander the Great.

Rhodes
ASIA MINOR
Cos
Miletus
Smyrna
Troy
Lesbos
AEGEAN SEA
Delos
Thera
Melos
Evros R.
Thasos
Philippi
MACEDONIA
Eretria
Pella
Thebes
Athens
OLYMPOS
Vergina
Delphi
Corinth
Mycenae
Sparta
Aliakmonas R.
Messene
Acheloos R.
Olympia
Ithaca
Dodona
Corfu
IONIAN SEA
CRETE
Knossos

FOREWORD

In the course of the last decades, a growing interest in the study of Greek antiquity has developed, that is not unrelated to the decline of moral standards and values, the unrestrained growth, and the incessant damage to our ecosystem. Modern man, under stress and frustrated, resorts to and draws upon the source of the enduring values of an eternal civilization such as ancient Greece.

However, most of our knowledge of Greek antiquity is based on the findings of archaeological research, which presents only part of the picture and which leaves us virtually ignorant of the ancient Greeks' everyday life.

What was their everyday life like? What were their eating habits? How did they entertain themselves? What was their love life like? Ignorance, misinterpretation and/or misleading information have led people astray, as is the case of the alleged Greek polytheism and of the so misunderstood sexual habits of the Greeks.

A lot of people would therefore like to learn more about the private life of the Greeks and of course about one of its principal expressions: *Eros.*[1]

What were their marriage customs? Did they get divorced? Was birth control practiced? What were their sexual preferences? What was pederasty really about? And what about prostitution?

This book will unpretentiously try to provide answers to all these as well as to other questions. Its purpose is to inform readers on what they may always have wanted to learn about sexual life in ancient Greece, in a simple, intelligible and documented way.

We have also included some erotic illustrations, as such representations are practically the only sources that can help us draw valuable conclusions on the sexual life of the Greeks. We have to clarify though, that in no case did these constitute the pornography of the times, as such a thing did not exist, since the Greeks were totally uninhibited in sexual matters.

---

[1] *Eros:* the feeling of intense attraction to something or someone, strong desire, passion, lust. In a broader sense: love.

1. *Votive monuments in the form of phalluses at the sanctuary of Dionysos in Delos, 3rd century* B.C. *(Photo: N. A. Vrissimtzis.)*

INTRODUCTION

The history of ancient Greece covers a period that starts from circa 4500 B.C. (Neolithic I) or even earlier,[1] and ends in 146 B.C. with the submission of the Greek cities to the Romans. Geographically speaking, the term "ancient Greece" covers not only contemporary Greek territory and Cyprus, but also the countries where the Greeks settled as colonists–the coastal region of Asia Minor, southern Italy and Sicily, Illyria, southern France, Spain, Libya, Egypt, Syria, the coasts of the Black Sea, as well as the countries conquered by Alexander the Great.

The historic period, from which written texts have come down to us, begins in the 8th cent. B.C. As a result,

2. *Aphrodite. Terra-cotta head from Corinth, Roman period (lost).*

---

[1] According to a theory, the Greeks had developed a universal civilization ruled by king Zeus, before 5000 B.C., that stretched as far as the Americas and the Indian peninsula. It was destroyed by the Flood of Deucalion, which took place before 3000 B.C., and the few survivors either ignored or were unable to draw upon the written accounts. Collective memory faded or was completely lost, and today only in certain myths and in some words of certain languages, can one trace its signs. Another flood is mentioned in the Greek mythology, that of Ogygus, probably caused by the melting of the glaciers in southern Europe (around 9000 B.C.).

we are inevitably forced to limit our retrospection to the historic times, and the boundaries of the present-day Greek territory. Our research covers society in Homeric times, and that of the historic period proper, from the 8th cent. B.C. until the fall of Greece to the Romans. This, however, doesn't prevent us from casting quick glances at other periods or other geographical territories for the sake of comparison.

Our only sources as far as the first period is concerned, are the Homeric poems, the *Iliad* and the *Odyssey*. Sources that are credible to the extent that literature can depict the customs and values of a given era, inadequate though when it comes to forming a complete picture of sexual relations.

For the second period, there is an abundance of written texts that facilitate the research. However, there is none among them that specifically deals with the subject of sexual life; thus, our information is extracted from literary texts, which certainly reflect to a fairly large extent the reality of their times. These include theatrical plays, historical, economic, political and philosophical texts, anthologies, poetry and even oratorical speeches, like for instance Demosthenes' *Against Neaera*,[2] recited in the 4th cent. B.C. against the prostitute Neaera; the latter was accused of having illegally obtained the status of an Athenian citizen's wife, despite the fact that she was foreigner; this was illegal, according to the law prohibiting mixed marriages.

Also, numerous representations have come down to us on every kind of vases; in particular, on nuptial vases, depicting the relevant customs and the wedding ceremony, and on kylikes ("drinking cups") concerning the sexual life itself; these illustrations provide us with invaluable information and important details not found in texts.

However, almost all the sources, texts and pictorial representations relevant to the subject are of Athenian origin, while corresponding testimonies from other Greek cities are either sparse or contradictory or unclear. We are thus, further restricted to what applied to and was practiced in Athens in the classical period (5th and 4th cent. B.C.). Nonetheless we should have no regrets, since most of what we have inherited from ancient Greece and upon which our modern culture is founded, has its origins in Athens of the same period. Besides, this restriction is dictated by a practical reason: every city-state was autonomous, with its own legislation and social structure and consequently different customs, values and traditions. In Sparta, for instance, where a totalitarian regime had been installed since the 7th cent. B.C., a completely different concept of marriage prevailed, as will be described later, while prostitution of any kind was unknown. In Sparta, also, whereas morals were generally strict, young girls trained together with boys and participated in athletics, something unheard of elsewhere.

Finally and most importantly, to understand the ancient Greek society and

---

[2] According to others, this speech is wrongly ascribed to Demosthenes; it is therefore attributed to an unknown orator, conventionally called Pseudo-Demosthenes.

its traditions, we have to approach it without prejudice, having previously discharged our own ethical code and our conception of what is ethically correct. It would be mistaken and also unfair to judge, using present-day criteria, a people and a civilization that flourished 2500 years ago, under particular geographic, political, social and economic conditions. Moreover, morality is fluid, as it is affected by various and different factors and often undergoes such radical changes, that something which today is regarded as immoral, may in another time be considered correct and vice versa. A case in point is the collapse of communism in eastern Europe. The drastic political changes that occurred, caused a tidal wave which swept away moral standards and the prevailing lifestyle which the society in question was based on.

3. *Terra-cotta figurines of Erotes (cupids) from the classical period. Museum of Pella, 1979.317, 1979.316.*

Hence, the noble institution of pederasty[3] shouldn't be confused or identified with homosexuality and pedophilia, the absence of taboos with immorality, the subordinate role of women in society with sexism and male chauvinism, the existence of slavery with racism, nor of course the Greek cult with polytheism and idolatry.

In particular, the Greeks regarded love and sex as something completely natural, as it should actually be. The difference between the ancient Greek conception and the contemporary one stems from the different nature of the ancient Greek cult[4] and the Christian religion. The latter which is based on the concept of guilt ("original sin"), has, since the beginning, considered the human body to be sinful and an incessant source of temptation that hampers the redemption of the soul. On the contrary, the Greek cult was based on a healthier concept, on the total acceptance of life and nature, and thus

---

[3] Pederasty: love of men for boys that did not necessarily have a sexual character. It is mostly recorded between the 6th and the 4th centuries B.C. among the upper class of Athens.

[4] It is conventionally called religion, although it wasn't really one, at least not according to our current conception of what a religion is. It was devoid of dogmas and didn't have sacred books, or a sacerdotal cast, or stereotyped rites and rituals. It was, on the contrary, a system of values, based on wisdom, moderation and harmony.

the worship of the body as the temple of the spirit and the soul, was believed in as an absolute value, always viewed of course as an inseparable part of the one and only whole–Nature, ("the Divine"). Accordingly, sexuality, which was more unrestrained than today, had, apart from its ideological and philosophical associations, a religious one, as, through the use of magical–sexual symbols and acts, it ensured and promoted the fertility of the earth and of women.

This sexual freedom is reflected in the folk-like form[5] of the Greek "religion": the Greek gods had a rich and varied love life, they had many lovers, and many children from various mates.

Unfortunately, the puritanical new religion that prevailed later, changed that concept and had a negative effect also on art: the Greeks had raised sculpture to a very high standard, creating beautiful and harmonious nudes, while the phallus, the magical-sexual symbol par excellence, with its fertilizing and apotropaic ("protective") powers was omnipresent.

The Christians however, having denied the beauty of the body and the pleasures of life, went as far as forbidding sculpture altogether. Indeed, after the 5th century, no sculptures are to be found, except for some non-pictorial religious ones.

The new ideal imposed on art, was that of the skeletal, sullen hermit. Beauty and Harmony had been expelled to eternal damnation!

Therefore, if we take these points into account, we can take a fresh look at and understand the deep, pure and true eroticism of this wonderful civilization. As *Eros* was for the Greeks the starting-point for everything!

4. *Bronze statuette of a Satyr from Dodona. End of 6th century B.C. National Archaeological Museum, Athens, KAP 22.*

---

[5] The famous Greek pantheon with its numerous gods and goddesses was nothing but the folk-like form of the Greek cult. In fact the ancient Greeks were the first to believe in one God. This is clearly discernible in the works of Plato, Aristotle and other philosophers, in the texts of the Orphics, and can also be deduced from a comparative study of philosophy, mythology, and history.

EROS & LOVE

We consider it necessary to clarify from the start that the English word *love* is translated into Greek either as *eros*, or *aghape*, two totally different concepts. The Greeks, who were pioneers in all and especially in philosophy, were also helped by their language, a rich and flexible one which could express the finest notions and nuances with exceptional ease. *Eros*, according to the dictionaries, is "an intense attraction to something or someone, a strong desire, lust," or according to Plato: "every intense desire for goods and happiness" *(Symposion)*. Derivatives of the word *eros* in English are: *ero*-genus or *ero*-genic = sexually sensitive; *ero*-tic = of or concerning sexual desire; *ero*-tica = erotic books, pictures etc. and *ero*-ticism = the state or quality of being erotic.

On the other hand, *aghape* means "deep fondness and affection." To be brief and

5. *Terra-cotta statuette of Eros from Corinth (lost).*

somewhat simplistic, *eros* corresponds to "I am in love" and *aghape* corresponds to "I love." The former includes passion and enthusiasm and the latter serenity and depth.

In the ancient texts, the use of the word *eros* is extensive and indeed not only when referring to human relations–there is *eros* for music, for philosophy, for art (Plato, *Symposion*). *Eros* is everywhere, it is the motivating force behind everything.

On the contrary, the word aghape was first used by the early Christians and indeed excessively. They called *aghapes* ("loves") the common dinners of the initiated, which, however, didn't have a liturgical character and often ended up in havoc, until finally Saint Paul condemned them and the Church prohibited them at the end of the 4th century.

6. *Aphrodite, Pan and Eros. Marble statue from Delos, circa 100 B.C. National Archaeological Museum, Athens, 3335.*

The Christians claimed that they enriched the ancient Greek thought with what the Greeks supposedly hadn't discovered up to then: aghape, meaning love, heartfelt acceptance, brotherhood. But not only did the concept exist, expressed by the words *philotis* ("love") and *philo* ("to love") but also, eros incorporated those as well as moral values in their entirety! Initiation through *eros* aimed at the revelation of the absolute Beauty ("the Divine") that stands by itself and is undivided and eternal: [the seeker of the truth, must, under the influence of eros]... "begin from the beauties of earth and mount upwards for the sake of that other beauty, using these as steps only, and from one beautiful body going to two, and from two to all fair forms, and from fair forms to fair practices, and from fair practices to fair notions, until from fair notions he arrives at the notion of the Knowledge which is no other than the revelation of the absolute Beauty" ["the Divine"] (Plato, *Symposion*).

We now have to clarify that, as far as human relations were concerned, the word *eros* was exclusively used to denote the relationship between men and youths, which was not necessarily sexual. This is due to the fact that marital relationships were deprived of sentiments like *eros* and love, as marriage was nothing more than a financial and social union with the purpose of preserving and continuing the *oikos*[1] ("house") and furthermore the *polis*[2] ("city-state"), and the race. The same concept is found in other ancient civilizations, but also in some contemporary ones, where love between husband and wife is not considered necessary, and it can even be undesirable! Thus, in the classical era, no marriages were entered into for love, neither in Athens, nor in the other Greek cities. This subject is however treated thoroughly in another chapter.

The deification of *eros* testifies to its importance for the Greeks. The god Eros was, according to Hesiod, a primordial deity of no known parentage, as old as Chaos and Earth (*Theogony* 116), which means that he was much older than Aphrodite, whose inseparable companion he is later depicted as being (Fig. 6). "The god Eros was the earliest and the most honored of the gods, since it was he who ensured virtue and prosperity during people's lifetime" (Plato, *Symposion*). Moreover, Hesiod refers to Eros as "the most beautiful of all immortals." How couldn't he be, since the Greeks adored beauty as the "most respected, most desirable, most divine of all values" (Isocrates).

7. *Eros (Cupid) in classical times was shown as a young man, rather than as a baby. Courtesy of "American School of Classical Studies at Athens: Agora Excavations."*

Eros was pictured winged, owing to the fact that he was very mobile and

---

[1] *Oikos:* house in its broader sense, meaning domicile, family and property.

[2] *Polis:* in its ancient meaning, a group of citizens, a city-state.

omnipresent as much on earth as in the sky. His power was enormous and nobody, neither god nor mortal, could resist him. He was actually considered dangerous, as he could make gods and men lose their reason, thus causing great disasters, such as the Trojan War.

The most important centers of his worship were Thespiai in Boeotia and Leuktra in Laconia, as well as the Sanctuary of the Muses on Mount Elikon. In addition, an altar and a statue of Eros stood at the entrance of the Academy of Athens,[3] as well as in all the gymnasia, next to the statues of Hercules and Hermes.

The god Eros had three brothers–Imeros, Pothos and Anteros (anti-Eros). The task of the latter was to punish those who did not respond to the love offered, or, according to another interpretation, Anteros was a divinity opposed to love. The same pictorial type was used for all four of them, and the distinction between them can only be made with the help of a possible inscription.

The illustrations of Eros were countless, while his place in poetry, philosophy and literature was prominent. We should note here, that Eros, as illustrated in the Greek classical period, doesn't bear the slightest resemblance to the chubby and mischievous little blond baby presented abundantly in Roman and Renaissance art. The Greek Eros was a dark-haired, vigorous and naked youth in his prime and full of grace, a fact that obviously reflects the spirit as well as the taste of those times (Fig. 7).

---

[3] Academy of Athens: a pleasant site, full of trees, on the outskirts of Athens, where Plato established his school of philosophy (387 B.C.– A.D. 529).

LOVE IN HOMERIC TIMES

There is no serious work about ancient Greece that doesn't start with Homer and his immortal epics.

The *Iliad* and the *Odyssey* raised and instructed countless generations of Greeks, as it was through these poems that they were taught reading and writing. As the orator Herakleitus writes: "From the earliest age the spirit of a child that learns for the first time accepts Homer as its nurture...We grow up and Homer is always by our side. We become men and he is still our lifelong companion. When we reach maturity, then we start to fully understand him. Never though, not even in our later years, will we feel the slightest satiety..."

Since then, Homer has instructed many generations of Europeans, up to the present day. And, while at the beginning he was believed to be and praised only as a poet (the greatest ever!), then came the discovery of Troy and Mycenae by Heinrich Schliemann to prove that Homer was also a historian and a sociologist, as his works were based on real events and as he superbly describes the customs and morals of his time.

We are therefore obliged to begin our exploration of the land of love with Homer and his poems. Besides, let's not forget that everything started when

8. *"The Ephebe of Antikythera." Probably a statue of Paris, the Trojan prince, who abducted Helen the queen of Sparta and thus caused the Trojan War. Bronze, 340 B.C. National Archaeological Museum, Athens, 13396.*

9. *The "Treasury of Atreus," or "Tomb of Agamemnon" at Mycenae. Circa 1350 B.C. (Photo: N.A.Vrissimtzis.)*

Helen, the queen of Sparta, fell in love with Paris (Fig. 8), the Trojan prince, and their flight to Troy. *Eros* was the motive and nobody can describe and praise it better than Homer!

In both poems we can observe that the world of gods and the world of mortals are somewhat connected and we read about gods falling in love as passionately as mortals. We follow Zeus' love affairs and his consequent fights with Hera, we learn about Aphrodite's infidelities, her affair with Ares and Hephaestus' revenge, and we admire the freedom of spirit with which the poet treats the gods. Obviously, the love life of the gods was much more free and exciting than that of the mortals, as was to be expected, after all!

If now we take a closer look at the world of the mortals, we can conclude that in the aristocratic, feudal society of the time, marriage was the rule, the institution upon which was founded the system for the management of the house, the creation of legitimate children-heirs and evidently the preservation of power. Testimony to the great importance of marriage and family in those times, are the numerous references to the wives and children of the heroes who had stayed back home.

In the Homeric poems, most heroes are married and although the epics in question mainly deal with the ruling aristocratic class, allusions found in them indicate that the same principles applied to the lower classes as well.

The dissolution of marriage occurred when one of the spouses left and married someone else like for example Helen and Paris, Klytemnestra and Aegisthus, whose new marriages were absolutely legal, despite the infidelity. In the *Iliad*, Helen is referred to as Paris' wife and not as his mistress!

Infidelity is certainly condemned and we learn of the suffering that it caused in particular instances: Agamemnon, was slain "like a bull in his stall" (Fig. 9) by his wife's lover (*Odyssey* iv, 535) and Klytemnestra was in turn punished in the same way by her son Orestes. On the contrary, Helen returned to Sparta, where she lived again as the lawful wife of Menelaus, despite the fact that she had caused a war and the death of countless people (Fig. 10).

Virginity as an anatomical detail was not required of young girls and the word virgin where found, only denotes young maidens, as virginity per se does not seem to be included in the qualities of a future bride. Pre-marital relationships existed, as we can deduce from references to young girls who had illegitimate children without this diminishing their moral or social status. Furthermore, the frequent and indeed favorable references to illegitimate children and their mothers, shows the tolerance of the morality of the time on this subject. Gods are of course credited with the paternity of these children, but in this case we should again consider the idealistic attitude of Homer.

Loyalty was required of married women not for moral reasons, but as a means of ensuring the legitimacy of the children. We can, on the other hand, observe the overt polygamy of men, especially when

10. *Menelaus and Helen. 580 B.C. Museum of Sparta, 1. (Photo: N. A. Vrissimtzis.)*

they are away from the house, on a trip or at war. This temporary infidelity, however, doesn't seem to threaten to destroy family or social peace. Moreover, loyalty is praised. A case in point is Penelope who waited for Ulysses for twenty whole years, resisting her suitors' advances. We have to note though that, when Ulysses was leaving for Troy, he told Penelope that if he wasn't back by the time their son Telemachus reached manhood, she could remarry. But she waited, with the secret hope that her husband would be back some day. And when Ulysses was sleeping with Calypso and Circe, his mind was set on Penelope and Ithaca! He remained faithful to her, at least mentally! We can't think of higher praise of marital faith than the *Odyssey*!

Parallel to marriage, was the custom of concubinage. When fighting a war in faraway lands, men weren't expected to suffer the deprivation of women! Thus, beautiful slaves from cities allied with Troy which the Greeks had seized, provided company and comfort for them! The most famous of such concubines were Chryseis and Briseis, the first belonging

11. *Golden funerary mask (of Agamemnon?) 16th century* B.C. *National Archaeological Museum, Athens, 624.*

to Agamemnon (Fig. 11) and the second to Achilles. Agamemnon went as far as declaring that more than his wife, he appreciated Chryseis, who was "younger, prettier, more educated and more competent." Achilles on the other hand said about Briseis: "she was nothing but a poor captive, but I loved her from the bottom of my heart." And when she was driven from Achilles to Agamemnon, she left "in spite of her heart" which shows that she had loved Achilles, although he had killed her husband and brothers.

As for Priamus, the king of Troy, it seems that he had a whole harem of concubines, as he had fifty sons and twelve daughters; apparently, neither his legal wife Hecuba, nor Laothoë could have given him so many children alone! As Lycaon said to Achilles: "...my mother Laothoë...the daughter of ancient Altes, was one of king Priam's numerous wives, and she bore me and another...my brother, Polydorus" (*Iliad* xxi).

It is well worth noting here that concubinage[1] was a useful practice, as a husband could have children in general, or boys in particular, if his legal wife was barren or if she only gave him girls. In that case, the legal wife had to tolerate the existence of the concubine. That was Menelaus' case: his wife, the beautiful Helen, only bore him a daughter, Hermione, and therefore he took a concubine by whom he had a son, Megapenthes.

It is noteworthy that in the Homeric poems no allusions to homosexuality are to be found. Ganymedes, the handsome Trojan youth who Zeus abducted and carried up to Mount Olympus, is mentioned only as the god's cup bearer (*Iliad* xx). The first time the myth acquired its supposed homosexual association, was in the 6th cent. B.C., in a poem by Theognis, according to which, Zeus abducted the youth because he had fallen in love with him.

---

[1] Concubinage: the custom according to which a woman who is not legally a wife, lives with a man and has a recognized position in his household, and who can coexist with the legal wife. Concubinage is a primordial institution which in some cases survived into the 20th century (see relevant chapter).

Similarly, there are no allusions to prostitution, which of course doesn't mean that the oldest profession was unknown, but it is more likely that the heroes found comfort in the company of concubines as mentioned above.

Although Homer doesn't offer us a lot of information about the love life in his times, it would appear that morality wasn't so strict, or at least not as strict as it would become later, in the classical era.

THE SOCIAL STATUS OF WOMEN

Obviously, love relationships at any place or period, are directly related to the social status of both sexes, and especially to that of women. In the ancient Greek society, women were deprived of civil rights, and, according to today's standards, their role was a subordinate one.

We should not, however, think that their position was unworthy. This would be totally wrong!

The Greeks gave to their women the roles nature had prescribed to them–that of the mother and that of the courtesan. Nothing more, nothing less!

And speaking about the role of the mother, we can say that it was every woman's goal; it was indeed the object of her life.

Her whole world was her house and her family. In her house she was the absolute mistress; as a mother she was respected not only by her husband and by her in-laws alike, but by everybody! The husband always honored his wife and mother of his children.

12. *Funerary monument of an Athenian woman: Hegesso, the daughter of Proxenos. National Archaeological Museum, Athens, 3624. (Photo: N. A. Vrissimtzis.)*

Speaking now on the details of the social status of women, we must say that they were not entitled to carry out any legal transactions; in particular, they could neither possess, nor buy or sell property. In these and in any other cases, the woman was represented by her "master," namely her father or husband or brother or finally her closest male relative. So, she was always under the protection of a man.

Women were not even registered in the official lists of the *Demos* or the *Fratria*[1]. The only rights this "passive" sort of citizen possessed were, first, that she could contract a legal wedding and bear legitimate descendants-heirs and second, the right of *epikleria*. In particular, when a daughter without a brother inherited from her father, she became *epikleros*, which literally meant that she "sat on the lot" (on the piece of land) without obviously being able to possess or manage or sell it, since, as we have already mentioned, she had no transaction rights. Therefore, the "heiress" was obliged to immediately marry her closest relative from her father's side, in order for the property to remain with the family.

Young girls didn't receive education, but learned from their mothers or from a maid, the management of the house, as well as weaving and occasionally, elements of reading, writing and arithmetic. It is obvious, though, that the girls of the lower classes had fewer chances of learning how to read or write. Only from the Hellenistic period onwards (323–30 B.C.), did girls start to attend schools.

Young women weren't allowed to show themselves in public, unless they were going to a religious or family gathering or to do their personal shopping; and even then they were always accompanied by their master or by a female slave. Even in their own houses, they were restricted to a special section, the *gynaekonitis*, usually located on the upper floor. This is what the much praised *sophrosyne* ("prudence") of the Greeks demanded of young women!

On the contrary, in Sparta girls engaged in physical activities in order to conform with the principle of eugenics of the Spartan regime. This shocked the Athenians, who called them *phainomirides*, as during exercise, their thighs were exposed (Euripides, *Andromache* 597). The choruses of young Spartan girls were also renowned.

We also know that on the island of Lesbos, at the beginning of the 6th cent. B.C., a pedagogical institute for young girls was established, under the direction of the famous and misunderstood poetess Sappho. But morals were more relaxed on that island–as well as in the other Aeolic cities and in Ionia[2]–as far

---

[1] *Demos:* a small or large self-governed territory and its inhabitants. At the beginning of the 5th cent. B.C., there were a hundred demoi in Attica. *Fratria*, was the union of several families of the same lineage to protect the common interests.

[2] Ionia: the coastal region of present-day Turkey in the Aegean Sea, between the rivers Ermos and Maiandros–and also the islands of Chios and Samos–that was inhabited by a large branch of the Greek nation, the Ionians, already by the 2nd millennium B.C.

13. *Funerary monument of Amphotto, a woman from Boeotia. 440 B.C. National Archaeological Museum, Athens, 739. (Photo: N. A.Vrissimtzis.)*

as women's education and conduct were concerned (see last chapter).

The young Athenian woman wasn't allowed to socialize with the opposite sex and she accordingly couldn't choose the man that she would marry. It was her legal master who would chose her future husband, even in spite of the wishes of the girl, whose consent wasn't necessary.

All marriages, irrespective of social classes, were unions of interest and expediency, and not of love.

The woman's position didn't change significantly after marriage, although she enjoyed a somewhat greater freedom of movement. Her master was now her husband and she carried on living in the house like before, except that now she was the one who managed it. In particular, she settled everything that had to do with everyday life. She saw to the upbringing of the children, supervised the slaves, took care of the provisions, supervised the handling, preservation and storage of agricultural and livestock products and also engaged in spinning and weaving in order to provide for the clothing needs of the family. She also kept the keys of the house, within which she was the indisputable mistress, a privilege that her husband could revoke at any time, however!

Both married and unmarried women only left their houses on special occasions, such as religious duties, personal shopping, ceremonies and of course always escorted. We should, though, clarify that this didn't strictly apply to all social classes. Occasionally, women of the lowest class were forced to work outside the home, owing to extreme poverty; they either sold their products in the market or worked mostly as weavers or seamstresses. But, working outside the home was only as a last resort.

Naturally, neighbors could exchange friendly visits to gossip or to borrow things from one another, but normally, a respectable woman should not be seen in public unless for a serious reason: "An honorable woman should remain within her house. The streets are for the unworthy" (Menander, *Fragment* 546). Even a short delay on her doorstep and the woman could be branded. As regards the everyday shopping, it was done by men or slaves. Furthermore, women, being excluded from public affairs as they were, found no interest in them and generally in whatever took place outside the home. Anything different would be considered at least improper as these were men's concern.

When guests were received at the house, the female members of the family didn't appear; servants looked after the guests under the supervision of the lady of the house. Women only participated in family gatherings. As a rule, the man always went out alone, not only to work or to participate in public affairs, but also to meet his friends and entertain himself in the palaestrae, in the games and in the symposia.[3]

Were women allowed to go to the theater? The answer to this question is yes, but they could most probably attend only tragedies. Considering the place of women in Athenian society, the strict morality and on the other hand the licentiousness and the foul language of comedies, we can say that a respectable woman never attended comedies. This is also asserted in Plato's *Laws* (658 d).

The woman's place in the society of the classical period, can be epitomized in the following excerpt from Demosthenes' speech *Against Neaera* (122): "We have the *hetairae*[4] ("courtesans") for pleasure, the concubines for the daily personal care and the legal wives to bear us children and manage our houses."

To sum it all up, we can say that the woman in ancient Greece not only lost the position she had held in the distant matriarchal society, but also the certain freedom she enjoyed in the prehistoric times (Minoan and Mycenean civilizations). However, we consider it important to clarify here, that the so-called matriarchal society wasn't the reverse of the

14. *The monument of the sisters Demetria and Pamphile at the ancient Athenian cemetery of Kerameikos. End of 4th century B.C. (Photo: N. A. Vrissimtzis.)*

---

[3] Symposia: dinners between men, followed by wine-drinking; they incorporated discussions and entertainment and sometimes wound up in orgies with the participation of the indispensable *hetairae*. The relevant works of Plato, Xenophon, Plutarch and others, were named after these.

[4] *Hetairae:* women of loose morals, distinguished from the common whores for their wit and skills. Their presence at the symposia was indispensable.

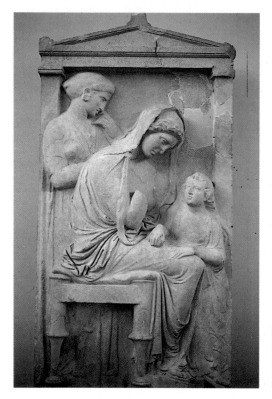

patriarchal, and the woman did not dominate the man, as it is often mistakenly believed. Matriarchy simply describes an age when the man's reproductive role was not clear and when it was believed that women created children by themselves. Consequently, the family line evolved around the woman and kinship and inheritance were matrilineal.

It is logical to wonder today, whether women were indeed unhappy leading that particular style of life. The answer is quite obvious: this was the only kind of life an honorable woman could live, and what one doesn't know one doesn't miss!

On the other hand, the man was polygamous, and the indisputable

15. Monument of Polyxene, circa 400 B.C. National Archaeological Museum, Athens, 723. (Photo: N. A. Vrissimtzis.)

master in a patriarchal society which can be described as the "most exclusive male club of all times." Not only did he enjoy full political and civil rights, but he also had absolute power over the female. He could at any time expel his wife–not without a reason and with some possible consequences, though; he could also, in spite of being married, keep one or more concubines, as described in the relevant chapter. He could, moreover, overtly entertain himself with the courtesans, wherever and whenever he pleased, without being called to account for his actions by anyone, much less by his wife!

MARRIAGE |

Marriage was regarded even from the prehistoric times, as the cornerstone of society. Family, through marriage, was the main core and the necessary condition for the preservation of the race. Thus, the value of marriage and family are praised in the Homeric poems and couples such as Zeus and Hera, Hector and Andromache, Ulysses and Penelope set the example, while single heroes like Achilles, Telemachus and Nausicaa, looked forward to getting married as soon as the war or their personal adventures were over.

In that distant time, there was no legal form of marriage, only unwritten rules that reflected the current traditions. It seems though, that there were at least two requirements that had to be fulfilled for a wedding to be lawful: first the *edna* had to be arranged and then the woman had to move to her husband's house in a formal procession. The *edna* were wedding presents which –as opposed to what became common later, in the classical era–the

16. *Nuptial procession of Herakles and his wife (Dianeira?). Large vase from Melos, 600 B.C. National Archaeological Museum, Athens, 354.*

groom-to-be gave to the bride's father as a sort of betrothal or wedding contract. These consisted of animals, expensive jewelry, woven cloths or other personal items, but not money, which at the time had yet to be invented! In case of separation on the woman's account, the edna was returned to the man, while if he was responsible for the separation, it remained with the woman's family. Obviously, this aimed to discourage separation, as the loss of the edna would be a considerable financial loss.

The second formality of the wedding–the introduction of the woman into her husband's home, and to his clan–came after the wedding feast which took place usually in the bride's maiden house. After the end of the feast and the subsequent settlement of the edna, the bride set off for her new home, in an ornamented carriage (Fig. 16). Musicians as well as relatives and friends holding torches and singing the *hymenaeus*, the wedding-song, formed the procession.

Unfortunately, that is all we know about marriage in this period, as, for lack of pictorial representations, our only sources of knowledge are the Homeric poems.

In the classical times now, marriage acquired a specific legal form which, in Athens, had probably been instituted by the legislator Solon (6th cent.

17. *Pericles. His relationship with Aspasia was notorious, almost scandalous for those times. (Photo: N. A. Vrissimtzis.)*

B.C.). For a marriage to be valid and legal, two requirements had to be fulfilled: the *engyesis* ("betrothal"), a sort of wedding contract between the future husband and the bride's father and the *ekdosis*, the handing over of the bride to the bridegroom's family. As long as the wedding was performed according to the above, the sons of the family could enjoy full hereditary, civil and political rights.

However, according to a law voted later, in 451 B.C., during Pericles' time, legal weddings were only considered those carried out not only in compliance with the aforementioned requirements but also exclusively between two Athenians. This law was dictated by political, social and economic reasons, as, on the one hand, the number of those claiming civil rights and access to power would be limited and on the other, the land wouldn't end up in the hands of foreigners.

Considering the fact that Athens had the leadership of the Athenian

League,[1] the aforementioned law was intended to prevent immigrants from city-allies of Athens from acquiring civil rights. As a result, mixed marriages, that is those between Athenians and foreign immigrants, which up to then had been legal, were thereupon considered free unions and male children born from them did not have political and civil rights.

A victim of this law was Pericles himself as, a year after it was voted he met the renowned Aspasia, a cultivated woman from Miletus. Pericles (Fig. 17) divorced his wife, who had given him two sons, and would have married Aspasia if she had been an Athenian or if she had originated from one of the allied cities which had been granted by Athens the right of *epigamy* (the right to marry Athenians). But, as this wasn't the case of Miletus, he lived with her the harmony of a free union, until his death in 429 B.C. She gave him a son who was deprived of political rights until Pericles managed to settle the matter with a special exception to the law.

For a citizen, the main reason to take a wife was to beget legitimate male children who would ensure the continuation of the family and would take care of him in his old age. Another motive for marriage was the union of two powerful or rich families and of their properties, in order to protect their common interests. It is therefore obvious that all marriages, at least until the 3rd cent. B.C., were unions of convenience.

As for the betrothed, they had probably never met before their engagement day. Besides, neither before, nor during nor after the wedding ceremony, was love or faith or devotion between husband and wife mentioned; everybody wished the newlyweds fertility and prosperity. Even sexual attraction between husband and wife was something rare, as it was common practice for men to sleep with their wives only for childbearing, and to satisfy their sexual needs out of the house with the courtesans. It has also been claimed that, after the creation of the desired number of descendants, the man wouldn't approach his wife sexually any more. Nonetheless, the nurturing of a deeper feeling between spouses wasn't excluded. Such an example is given by Xenophon in his *Symposion* (8, 3), where Socrates says: "Nikiratos, from what I've been told, really loves his wife and she loves him, too."

Marriages were thus arranged by the parents, namely the fathers and, where there was no father, the closest male relative took charge. The choice of husband was made according to the aforementioned criteria and relatives were not ruled out.

We should note here though, that whereas it was forbidden for children who had the same mother to get married, it was nevertheless acceptable if they had the same father, but a different mother. Among others, is mentioned the case of Themistocles' daughter from his second marriage, who

---

[1] Athenian League: military alliance between many Greek islands and coastal cities of the Aegean Sea and Athens, established in 478 B.C. Its headquarters was initially Delos and later Athens.

married her half-brother from the great statesman's first marriage. Furthermore, Demosthenes mentions that his grandfather had married his half-sister who had a different mother. Finally, Pericles himself, was married to a relative of his. It was also possible for a girl to marry her uncle. Such marriages however, were only solutions of necessity, when the family property had to be saved: the epikleros ("heiress"), for lack of a brother from the same father, had to marry her father's closest relative in order for the land to remain within the family.

Refusal on the part of the children to accept their parents' choice, was out of the question, not only for reasons of obedience, but also because marriage was for them an inescapable reality and not the means for their personal happiness. As the poet Menander states: "Marriage is the necessary evil" (*Fragment* 651).

Women were marriageable at about 16 and men at about 30. Let's listen to Hesiod's advice: "You are of age to marry a wife and bring her home with you when you are about thirty, not being many years short of that mark, nor going much over. That age is ripe for marriage. Let your wife be full grown four years, and marry in the fifth" (Hesiod, *Works and Days* 695-699). Although there was no legal form to regulate this issue, it seems no marriages of girls before puberty took place—as was practiced later in Rome—nor did young men get married before they had fulfilled their military duties. Marriage was of utmost importance for the State and, accordingly in Athens, whoever exceeded the age of forty and was still single, had to pay a special "bachelor" tax; a similar law in Sparta, imposed by Lycurgus, punished unmarried men (Plutarch, *Lycurgus* 15).

18. *Terra-cotta statuette of Aphrodite and Eros from the Hellenistic period. Museum of Veroia, Π 3109.*

Another important difference between the classical and the Homeric era, was the chastity of young girls. According to a law of Solon, young girls were obliged to safeguard their virginity until they got married. The intention of keeping this required virginity also accounts for the girls' young age of marriage.

The engyesis, as mentioned above, was an unwritten nuptial

agreement, a sort of wedding contract of great validity. We can say that a marriage took effect from the moment of the engyesis, while the ekdosis, the handing over of the bride, which followed was nothing but the ratification of an already established fact. The engyesis, important as it was, took place before the family altar, where, in front of witnesses, the groom-to-be and his future father-in-law, shook hands and exchanged few, but formal and ceremonial words which took the form of a vow! And it is certainly well known how far the Greeks honored their vows! The bride, if present, was a silent participant, while the presence of the bridegroom's father is uncertain, but it is unquestionable that the son had previously ensured his father's approval.

An inseparable part of the engyesis was the *proika* (dowry): apart from the official promise given by both parties, a nuptial donation was arranged, which the bride's father would give to the bridegroom as a sort of indemnity for his daughter's living expenses as she was not supposed to work. The parties involved agreed and determined the sort, the means and the time of payment of the dowry.

There were two reasons for this custom (which is still practiced in Greece, although officially abolished in 1981) –to attract and to deter. On the one hand, it attracted men with the opportunity of increasing their personal property and correspondingly multiplied the women's chances for marriage, and on the other, it deterred divorces, as in such case, the dowry reverted to the bride's family. The dowry had to be returned even in case of the husband's death and was given to the one who would look after the woman thereupon–her children or her father's family or for lack of them, her closest relative.

In the historic times, the dowry could consist of money or real estate or both. In the classical era, as we learn from the sources the dowry of an Athenian girl ranged between a thousand and five thousand drachmas, a substantial amount of money, if we take into account the fact that a little before Pericle's death, the wages for a day's work were one drachma, a sum sufficient to cover the daily expenses of a family of four. There were of course richer families that endowed their girls accordingly, and cases are mentioned of dowries reaching the amount of two *talanta*[2] (twelve thousand drachmas) or even more, as, for example the dowry that Alcibiades received–twenty talanta (Plutarch, *Alcibiades* 8). The amount of the dowry wasn't regulated by law, but was the outcome of free negotiations between the two parties. This custom was of such great significance, that the State itself provided the dowry for the girls of the poor citizens. A law formulated especially for the financially weaker class of the landless obliged the relatives of a girl without means, to raise a dowry for her.

Evidently, another purpose of the dowry was to unite financial interests,

---

[2] *Talanton* (pl. *talanta* = talents), a unit of value: 1 talanton = 100 drachmas. Also measure of weight, equal to twenty-six kilograms.

19. *A bride being adorned for her wedding. Nuptial lebes, circa 420 B.C. National Archaeological Museum, Athens, 14790.*

through the merging of powerful families, but also to redistribute wealth among the less powerful ones.

The husband who received the dowry, could administer it at will and without any restrictions as if it were his, due to the fact that, as we have already seen, the woman was deprived of the right to possess or manage property. Therefore, the law which stipulated the return of the dowry in case of divorce or death was only of relative value, since the husband could have meanwhile wasted the money, or sold the land. In that case, if the impoverished woman wished to remarry, she had to collect a new dowry, or to be precise, her relatives had to do it for her.

During the negotiations for the engyesis, the date of the wedding, or more precisely of the ekdosis (the handing over of the bride), was arranged as well, and usually followed soon after. Most weddings were performed in the month of *Gamelion*³ as this month was dedicated to Hera, the patron goddess of marriage; the couples, however, that couldn't wait for one reason or another, chose the time of the full moon of another month.

A day before the wedding, two important rituals took place–the sacrifices, and the purification of the future spouses. First, the bride's father sacrificed to Zeus and Hera, Aphrodite, Artemis and Peitho,⁴ divinities that were associated with marriage. Zeus and Hera weren't merely the most prominent divinities of the Greek Pantheon, but they also epitomized the perfect couple, in spite of Zeus' infidelities and his notorious fights with Hera. Aphrodite was of course the goddess of love, but also of fertility. Artemis symbolized puberty which the future wife was leaving behind, while as Artemis Eilei-

---

³ *Gamelion:* the 7th month of the Attic calendar, corresponding to January–February.

⁴ The Muse Peitho, or according to others Hera Peitho, or Aphrodite Peitho.

thyia she would also later protect the woman in labor. Lastly, the sacrifice to Peitho set the foundations (obedience, understanding) upon which the marriage should be based. In another ritual, the bride-to-be dedicated to Artemis certain items related to her childhood and adolescence which she was now abandoning, like her toys and other personal belongings–mirrors, hair ties, hair nets, etc. The wedding custom of offering some locks of the girl's hair to Artemis, was practiced in Delos (Herodotus 4, 34), in Troezen and in Megara (Pausanias, *Graeciae Descriptio* i, 43, 4 and ii, 33, 1). The sources include no testimonies for Athens. It is nonetheless obvious, that this custom symbolized the transition from adolescence to maturity. There was no similar custom or sacrifice for grooms-to-be given the fact that, by the time of their marriage, they had already reached the age of thirty, having consequently left puberty far behind.

Of great significance was the custom of the future spouses' purification, that is the ceremonial bath taken before the wedding. In Athens, the bride bathed in water from the spring Kallirrhoe, the best known spring of the city (Thucydides ii, 15). A procession known as *loutrophoria*, set off from the bride's house and headed for the spring. It consisted of a young boy playing the flute, most probably the son of the bride's closest relative and of friends and relatives who held torches; one of them carried the *loutrophoros*, a special vase with a high neck and two handles, which would be filled with water from the spring. It remains unclear whether the bride participated in the procession, as she appears only in few such illustra-

20. *Preparation of the bride before the wedding. 4th century B.C. State Hermitage Museum, Saint Petersburg.*

tions on vases, like as, for example on one kept in the National Archaeological Museum of Athens (1453).

On a vase, in the Warsaw Museum, a young man is depicted having his ceremonial bath before the wedding, but it is more likely that men purified themselves bathing in rivers, something that was inappropriate for a woman to do.

Evidently, this ceremonial bath, apart from purification, had also another symbolic character: just as the river and the spring water and fertilize the earth, it would similarly contribute to the fertility of the newlyweds. Let's not forget here, that the belief in the magic power of water is to be found in every known civilization and religion. Let's remember the deification of the river Acheloös, the baptism in the Jordan, the holy Nile, the "immortal waters" of the Styx, the holy river Ganges, where the living are purified and where the ashes of the dead are laid, the custom of the Muslims of washing before prayer, and so on. Besides, let's also not forget that the human body consists of water in its greatest part, as does Earth; therefore water was always considered almost "holy."

We should mention that loutrophoroi were put on unmarried women's and men's graves, to emphasize the fact that they had died before marrying. What differentiated these funeral loutrophoroi from those used in the weddings was that they had a thicker neck and occasionally three instead of two handles.

The following day saw the last phase of the rituals and the conclusion of the wedding with the ekdosis,[5] the handing over of the bride. First, a glorious dinner was given in the house of the bride's father, which was decorated with olive branches and laurels. All the relatives and friends participated, and the women sat at separate tables. The celebration also included music by professional musicians (Lucian, *Symposion*).

The bride was accompanied by the *nympheftria*,[6] a good friend of hers who held her veil. Customarily, the bride was covered with a veil from head to toe, with only a small opening for the eyes and which she was to take off only after the end of the meal (Lucian, *Symposion* 8). According to one interpretation, the veil protected her from the Evil Eye, until the conclusion of the wedding.

The bridegroom, crowned with a wreath, was escorted by his best friend, the *parochos* (a sort of best man).

A youth, adorned with thorns and oak-leaves, the *pais amphithales*, chosen only if both his parents were alive, carried around a basket and offered bread to the guests, pronouncing these symbolic words: "I have avoided evil, I found what is better." The meaning of this was that the newlyweds passed

---

[5] *Ekdosis:* a derivative of the verb *ekdidomai* (to grant, to yield, to concede) which means the concession of a thing or right from the jurisdiction of someone to that of somebody else. Its use implies that the bride was nothing more than a piece of property, at the disposal of her father's authority.

[6] *Nympheftria:* bridesmaid. This custom is still extant in Greece, as well as that of the veil as an accessory of the wedding dress.

from puberty into maturity and from a primitive way of life to a more civilized one (marriage), which was here symbolized by bread, the product of the cultivation of the earth and an eternal symbol of the values of civilization.

After the end of the meal, and before the bride was taken to her husband's house, the ceremony of the *apokalypteria* ("un-

21. *Unveiling the bride (Apokalypteria). Loutrophoros, circa 430 B.C. National Archaeological Museum, Athens, 16279.*

veiling") took place (Fig. 21): the nympheftria, pulled the bride's veil and revealed her. The guests then applauded and offered her presents, which were also called *apokalypteria*.

Afterwards, the couple got into an ornamented carriage, pulled by oxen or horses and the procession set off for the bridegroom's house. The bridegroom drove the carriage while on his left sat the bride, holding either a wreath of flowers, or a cradle, the symbol of her married life thereafter. The bride was now uncovered, as the main reason for this procession, called *nymphagogeia*, was to make the wedding public, while also symbolizing the bride's passage from her father's to her husband's authority.

The carriage proceeded slowly, led by the torch-bearer and followed by relatives and friends who were singing the hymenaeus, the wedding-song, to the accompaniment of flutes.

When the newlyweds reached the bridegroom's house, his parents welcomed them, his father crowned with myrtle and his mother holding a torch.

As the couple were getting out of the carriage, the participants sprinkled the bride with dried figs and walnuts, and offered her a piece of the wedding cake made of sesame and honey, as well as a quince. The latter sym-

22. In front of the bride's bedroom, the next day after the wedding. From the wedding of Alkestes and Admettus. Epinetron, 425 B.C. National Archaeological Museum, Athens, 1629.

bolized love and fertility, being associated with the cult of Aphrodite. Then, the bridesmaid guided the bride around the hearth (the family altar) and subsequently to the nuptial chamber. The door closed and the marriage was consummated.

One of the bridegroom's friends stood outside the room all night as a guard, while the bride's friends sang a nuptial song, the *epithalamion*, and made noise in order to ward off the evil spirits.

What happened in the room after the door had closed, is not to be found in the texts, nor in any pictorial representation. The reason for this is obvious and understandable. An honorable Athenian woman's private life couldn't come out in public, nor her name be publicly mentioned, as strange as this may sound. This rule was so strictly applied that not even in oratorical speeches do we encounter Athenian women's names, while the ones mentioned are exclusively those of prostitutes or slaves. The same was true of illustrations.

It has to be made absolutely clear that all non-mythological erotic representations, on any vases of any period, picture exclusively women of loose morals and slaves. No respectable women were ever pictured anywhere.

Besides, there was nothing sensual about marital sex as it was simply intended for procreation and not for pleasure (Xenophon, *Memorabilia* ii, 2, 4).

Nevertheless, there are a few vases which show the newlyweds in the bridal chamber, not in some sexual embrace though.

The following day, songs woke up the newly wedded pair, and the bride's parents as well as other relatives arrived with presents (Fig. 22).

When finally the celebrations of the day were over, they thanked the gods associated with marriage and especially Hera and Aphrodite, without though excluding others, and dedicated the loutrophoros used in the wedding, to the sanctuary of the Nymphs[7] on the south slope of the Acropolis. The celebrations lasted for two or three more days and ended with the registration of the wedding in the lists of the fratria. There, two witnesses had to verify that the bride was the daughter of a legal marriage between two Athenians, in order for her children to be entitled to civil and political rights.

In Sparta, the wedding was performed as follows: "The man carried off a maiden who was at the proper age for marriage. The bridesmaid received the maiden who had been carried off, shaved her head close, dressed her in a man's dress and shoes and left her alone in a dark room, lying on a straw mattress. The bridegroom left his army barracks after he had taken a meal with his table-companions, and, taking all precautions, entered the room where the bride was and after undressing her, carried her to another bed. He spent a short time with her and then he went away again quietly, back to his army companions. The same procedure was repeated every time he wanted to sleep with his wife! (Plutarch, *Lycurgus* 15).

Up to this point, two important things have become clear: first, neither before nor during the various ceremonies, was there the slightest hint of spiritual union and/or love between the spouses and second, marriage wasn't sanctioned by religion and likewise neither was birth nor death.

The absence of this last element, otherwise common to all known religions, lends weight to the theory that the so-called ancient Greek religion wasn't a religion at all, at least not according to our current conception of what a religion is.

As we have already mentioned, the woman's life didn't significantly change after marriage.

She carried on living in the house and looking after the household, while the man was responsible for his business and for bringing money into the family. When the man invited his friends to the house, his wife wouldn't participate.

The man visited his friends, the agora, the courts, and the sporting grounds, alone. The couple very seldom ate together, as the man spent most of his day away from the house. Moreover, they slept apart, the women in the gynaekonitis and the men in the *andron*. Besides, they didn't have a lot to talk about, except for trivialities and matters concerning the family, owing to her being uneducated and withdrawn and his being cultivated and social.

Their sexual life, focused on procreation rather than pleasure and therefore they only copulated for this purpose. It is thus clear, that sex was of minor importance in the marriage and this also explains the fact that there are no relative references in the sources.

Another reason is that the strict morality of the period didn't allow descriptions or representations of honest women during sexual intercourse.

---

[7] Nymphs: divinities concerned with the protection of springs, forests, caves and mountains. They were represented as young, beautiful and kind-hearted girls.

Of course, the man indulged his sexual drive elsewhere, with the *hetairae* and prostitutes, unrestrained and at will, and with the definite tolerance of society. On the contrary, the sexual needs of the woman depended on her husband's desire (actually on what was left of it, after all his extramarital activities), as for her there was no alternative.

As a counterbalance to that oppression, chastity was raised to the highest virtue for women and was indeed required of them, not for moral reasons though, but to ensure the legitimacy of the children.

Be that as it may, there were still women who cheated on their husbands!

DIVORCE

For a Greek husband there was no such a thing as infidelity in marriage. To be deprived of aesthetic and sensual enjoyment because he was married was beyond his logic. The society and the morals of the times recognized the polygamous nature of the man, who of course acted accordingly!

There were however voices, although really few, who preached for a like morality between husband and wife (Aristotle, Isocrates, Plautus).

But what happened in the case of adultery on the woman's part? There was of course the solution of divorce.

To start with, the woman's adultery always resulted in her expulsion from her husband's house, as such conduct couldn't guarantee the legitimacy of his descendants and finally led to the dissolution of marriage. Adultery was the most severe insult against a man's honor and also against his right of possession. Let's not forget that the Trojan War was fought to save Menelaus' honor!

Honor and disgrace were two concepts that carried much weight in ancient Greek society. The husband's honor was of such importance that, according to an old Drakon's[1] law, in a case where the husband caught the adulterers in the act and killed his wife's lover, he was acquitted! It seems that the same law was still in effect in the classical period, as it is mentioned in the case of a certain Euphiletus who, informed of his wife's infidelity, watched her and catching the adulterers in the act, killed her lover Eratosthenes; later in the trial the orator spoke in his defense (Lysias, *De Caede Eratosthenis*). Furthermore, Aristotle in his *Athenians' State* (57, 3) informs us that the same law was still in effect in his time.

The adulterer could get away with a fine at best and with *rap-*

---

[1] Dracon: Athenian legislator (7th cent. B.C.), the first to institute written laws, which were so strict that the word was they had been written in blood.

anismos at worst, that is the penalty of having a radish inserted in his rectum! *(Suïdas)*. Nevertheless, those who apparently knew all the ropes or had great influence got away unpunished. A case in point is Alcibiades (Fig. 23) who, when exiled in Sparta, got involved with king Agis' wife, Timaia, and a child she bore nine months later was supposedly his (Athenaeus xii, 535 b). Alcibiades again, when his wife, Hipparete, left him and the divorce was issued at his expense, took her back by force ignoring the decision of the authorities and escaping punishment.

According to Solon, the legislator, a woman caught in the act of adultery: "...may not put on ornaments and may not visit the public temples, lest she should corrupt innocent women; but if

23. *Alcibiades perhaps the most controversial political figure of Athens was also known for his notorious love life. Mosaic, Hellenistic period. Museum of Sparta, 11582.*

she does so or adorns herself, then any man who meets her may tear her clothes from her body, strip her of her ornaments, and beat her; but he may not kill her or make her a cripple" (Aeschines, *Against Timarchus* 183).

The expulsion of the adulteress and the consequent divorce, however, meant that the husband had to return the dowry to her family and suffer substantial financial loss. Thus, some deceived husbands swallowed their pride (and the insult), and accepted their wives' repentance.

However, adultery wasn't the only ground for divorce. A man could divorce his wife for many reasons, like, for example infertility. And for this to be done, he had to plead it in front of two witnesses. For the woman though, divorce on her own initiative was a harder process, as, legally disadvantaged as she was, she couldn't start legal proceedings herself.

She had to address the *Archon*[2] and give a written account of the reasons for which she wanted divorce. The Archon would then order an inquiry to prove the truth of her statements and then issue his decision.

Obviously, from what has already been said, the woman could not cite her husband's adultery, however overt, as grounds for divorce. Proven physical abuse or beating by her spouse on the other hand could result in divorce. As a result of the divorce proceedings, however, the woman's name would be discussed publicly, and this was most undesirable. Divorced women, although not excluded from remarrying, were treated with suspicion.

For Sparta, where the legislation as well as morals were different, Plutarch gives us the following characteristic story: "Geradas, an old Spartan, being asked by a foreigner, how the Spartans punished adulterers, replied: 'there are no adulterers among us.' 'But if there should be?' 'Then, as a punishment, he'll have to give a bull large enough to stretch out his head over Mount Taygetus.' 'Wherever in the world could so big a bull be found?' And Geradas replied: 'How could there be an adulterer in Sparta?!'" (Plutarch, *Lycurgus* 15).

We should also notice the following practice: according to a law of Lycurgus,[3] an elderly or infertile husband could introduce a young man to his wife, in order to beget especially beautiful and vigorous children, without the marriage being thereby upset. Furthermore, a man of noble descent, who appreciated a married woman's virtues, could ask her husband's permission to copulate with her, so as for the city to obtain strong children of excellent race (Ibid.).

This law apparently stemmed from the philosophy of eugenics that prevailed in Sparta and determined the ethics of marriage and birth, but led, as an additional effect, to the absence of jealousy between spouses.

Also, if a Spartan man had enough children with his wife, it was common for him to offer her to one of his friends for copulation (Polybius).

But of course all that was not considered adultery.

In Athens, and also elsewhere, if the husband faced a serious problem with his wife, such as if she was infertile or if she couldn't give him sons, but didn't want to divorce her so as to keep the dowry, then he resorted to concubinage.

---

[2] *Archon:* high official who, among other duties, was in charge of the affairs of those who were deprived of civil rights.

[3] Lycurgus: Spartan legislator who lived and administered in the 8th century B.C. According to others, he was a mythical person.

THE CONCUBINES

he institution of concubinage dates back to the earliest times and is found in every ancient civilization of the broader Mediterranean region. Let us remember the case of Abraham, who, incited by his wife, Sarah, took as his concubine the Egyptian maid Agar with the purpose of having children with her: "Now Sar'ai, Abram's wife, bore him no children. She had an Egyptian maid whose name was Hagar; and Sar'ai said to Abram, 'Behold now, the Lord has prevented me from bearing children; go in to my maid; it may be that I shall obtain children by her.' And Abram hearkened to the voice of Sar'ai. So, after Abram had dwelt ten years in the land of Canaan, Sar'ai, Abram's wife, took Hagar the Egyptian, her maid, and gave her to Abram her husband as a wife" (Genesis 16, 1–3, *The Holy Bible,* Revised Standard Version).

But, apparently, Abraham had more than one concubine: "Abraham took another wife, whose name was Ketu'rah. She bore him Zimran, Jokshan, Medan, Mid'ian, Ishbak, and Shuah" (Ibid., 25, 1). "Abraham gave all he had to Isaac. But to the sons of his concubines Abraham gave gifts, and while he was still living he sent them away from his son Isaac, eastward to the east country" (Ibid., 25, 5).

So it would seem, that often, especially if the concubine was intended for childbearing, the lawful wife gave her consent. But, that wasn't always the case. From Homer *(Iliad)*, who often refers to concubines, we learn that the concubine of king Amyntor, the father of Phoenix, was at the center of a serious family tragedy. Amyntor appreciated his concubine a lot more than his wife and the latter, in order to take revenge, but also to protect her rights, put her son up to seducing and copulating with the concubine, so she would loathe the old man. Phoenix did what his mother had asked, but when Amyntor found out, he cursed his son; as a result, Phoenix left the house to avoid patricide and found shelter at Peleas' house.

This primordial institution, was still extant at the beginning of this century in some Greek regions, while it is still practiced in some oriental nations.

The main aim of concubinage was childbearing, in cases where the legal wife was infertile or only bore girls, and therefore it was considered lawful and apparently desirable by the State. In Athens during the Peloponnesian War[1] married Athenian citizens were encouraged (if not obliged) to take a concubine each, even a foreign one, so as to, with the increase of legal births, make up for the great losses of the war *(Suïdas)*.

Even Socrates himself (Fig. 24), had, apart from his legal wife Xanthippe, one more, whose name was Myrto (Diogenes Laertius). For the same reason, another law accepted as legal all the weddings that had been performed without respect to the required formalities, as well as all the free unions between Athenians and foreign women.

The concubines were free women or *metoikoi* and seldom slaves. The metoikoi

24. *Statue of a philosopher (Socrates?). 3rd century B.C. Museum of Delphi, 1819.*

were immigrants from other cities and as such, were deprived of political rights; furthermore, from 451 B.C. onwards they weren't allowed to marry an Athenian man or woman. For the same reason Pericles couldn't marry Aspasia who was a foreigner, and so kept her as his concubine (Fig. 25). Into the same category, fell the freedmen and freedwomen (slaves that had gained their freedom). Thus, concubinage was often the only way out for foreign women.

Athenian women now, resorted to concubinage only due to extreme poverty and especially for lack of dowry. The father who was unable to collect a dowry for his daughter gave her as a concubine usually to a wealthy citi-

---

[1] Peloponnesian War: the war between Athens and Sparta and their respective allies, that started in 431 and ended in 404 B.C. with the defeat of Athens.

zen, having previously elicited the promise of financial compensation in case of separation.

The children of the concubines were considered legal and as proof to that we'll mention a law, invoked by Demosthenes: "If one kills a man caught committing adultery with his wife, or sister, or daughter, or concubine kept for the creation of legitimate children, then he is not exiled as a murderer."

25. *Aspasia. The controversial companion of Pericles.*
(Photo: N. A. Vrissimtzis.)

CONTRACEPTION AND FAMILY PLANNING

Even though the problem of overpopulation, as the term is understood nowadays, didn't exist at the time, most families didn't desire a large number of children, in order for the family's lot not to be divided into many shares. Furthermore, girls were evidently less welcomed than boys, as on the one hand they couldn't work and produce and on the other, they had to be given a dowry which reduced the family's property.

Plato in his *Laws* mentions two as a satisfactory number of children–a boy and a girl.

Obviously, accidental pregnancy was undesirable not only for married women, but also for the hetairae and the prostitutes.

To cope with that problem the Greeks practiced protection during intercourse, and abortion, but also infanticide and abandonment of the infant to the elements, if the other methods had proved unsuccessful.

Hippocrates (Fig. 26), the father of medical science (460–377 B.C.), was opposed to abortion (unless the pregnant woman's health was in danger) and advised, if pregnancy was to be avoided, that copulation took place during the infertile days of the menstrual cycle. Another method was copulation during menstruation. Let's note here that the Greeks didn't regard sexual contact during menstruation as something impure of which they would later have to be purified.

Apart from some medicines and

26. *Hippocrates, the father of medical science (460–377 B.C.). Marble, late Hellenistic period. Museum of Cos, 32.*

poisons with sperm-killing properties or alleged contraceptive qualities (e.g. sulfurous iron, carbonic lead, etc.) they tried magic spells. According to Dioscorides *(Materia Medica),* if a pregnant woman stepped on the root of the cyclamen, she would abort. Again according to the same writer, the root of asparagus, worn as an amulet, would turn somebody barren (Ibid., 151). Pliny, informs us that the egg of the raven, if eaten by a pregnant woman, caused abortion! *(Historia Naturalis* x, 32).

Another widespread contraceptive method, popular to these days, was that of interrupted intercourse (Soranus 1, 45).

Given that the extra-marital affairs of men were sufficient to satisfy or even satiate their sexual desires, sexual intercourse with their wives was, as a rule, not frequent. However, in case of accidental pregnancy, the woman had to choose between deliberate miscarriage (by trying magic spells, by doing heavy work or bodily exercise) and abortion. And, although it was for her to make a decision in the case of unwanted pregnancy, especially for abortion, her husband's consent–or her master's if she was a slave–was indispensable.

There was no law against abortion and the State only intervened when it was a question of protecting the rights of the woman's master, whether she was free or slave. Nevertheless, due to the fact that it was difficult to enforce this, unauthorized abortions took place, as they do today.

As for abortion considered from a moral point of view, Plato *(Republic* 461), maintained that the fetus wasn't a human being, but became one after birth, thus justifying it as acceptable and legal. Aristotle, on his part, advised that the abortion should only take place before the fetus acquired life and feeling, meaning its first movements *(Politics* 4, 14, 10).

From the moment a child was born and was unwanted, either because it was illegitimate or because the family already had enough and one more would be a burden, there were two ways for the parents to get rid of it–to put it to death or to abandon it. Moreover, while infanticide was forbidden and punished by law, there was no legislation to prevent the abandonment of infants. Besides, even though infanticide constituted a criminal act, it was still practiced.

In Sparta, it was indeed the task of the State to do it, for different reasons though: the new-born babies were presented to the committee of the Senators who examined them; the ill-born and deformed were thrown into the *Apothetae,* a deep cavern near Mount Taygetus, where the Spartans also threw those sentenced to death (Plutarch, *Lycurgus* 16). Yet another expression of the Spartan eugenics!

However, a more widespread method of doing away with unwanted babies, was to abandon them, which in most cases resulted in their death through starvation or lack of care. Anyhow, this was done soon after birth and had to be before the tenth day, when, in Athens, the child was given a name, since only from that moment was the child considered to exist officially.

Evidently, in both cases of killing and abandonment, most victims were either illegitimate children or baby girls. The few that survived being abandoned, were automatically considered slaves, and the girls ended up in prostitution. Some children were luckier though, as they were brought up by people who had found and wanted to keep them for some reason.

Lost children frequently provided the subject matter for the New Attic Comedy, and considering the fact that the literature of a period reflects, up to a certain extent, the reality of the time, we can conclude that abandonment of infants was a widespread practice.

27. *A vase showing two couples making love: the couple at the bottom are copulating anally. 450 B.C. Museum of Kerameikos, 1063. Deutsches Archäologisches Institut Athen.*

SEX

A number of things concerning the sexual habits of the ancient Greeks have been misunderstood, either due to misinterpretation of the sources, or to biased Christian morality.

Various writers, scholars and archaeologists who often disagree over a subject, putting forward theories that are frequently diametrically opposed and conflicting, have also contributed to this.

Thus, the student as well as the average reader, are often torn between two or more theories, presented in such a way that each one of them can be equally convincing. Illustrative are the examples of the controversy over the origin of the Greeks, that of the origin of the Greek alphabet, as well as the alleged homosexuality of the ancient Greek society.

We will thus try here to present our opinion on this controversial issue of the sexual habits of the Greeks.

Our principal sources of information are literature and more importantly, pictorial representations. Plenty of vases, dating mostly between the 6th and the 4th century B.C., have come down to us depicting the sexual preferences of the Greeks.

When looking at these illustrations, one wonders: is it mere pornography? Is there any kind of symbolism or religious character hidden behind all this?

To begin with, there were vases of religious-devotional character, mostly associated with fertility (both animal and vegetable), others had an apotropaic role (warding off evil), still others were indeed intended to provide sexual stimulation. There were finally some vases whose main purpose was humorous and where the artist painted his fancy, depicting mostly mythical creatures copulating in every possible way.

The first category concerns vases of religious intention depicting the Holy Matrimony, i.e. couples of humans or animals, copulating; they were offered to shrines or temples with the supplication for the fertility of a woman, a herd or a field. The Holy Matrimony was a rural ritual aiming to ensure fertility, and was associated with the cult of Dionysos. Moreover, the Satyrs and the *Sileni*[1]–mythical beings, companions of Dionysos, who were always depicted with an erection–were also symbols of fertility. Let us remember here that all ancient religions were extremely concerned with fertility, as all ancient societies were agricultural.

The second category concerns vases which, through illustrations of the phallus, aimed at warding off evil. It was a common belief that the phallus and the eye[2] possessed apotropaic powers over the Evil Eye, and accordingly people used both as amulets. Athens was full of *herms,* marble pillars with elaborate head (of Hermes, or other gods later) and a phallus (Fig. 28). The herm may have derived from some primordial non-pictorial representation of Hermes. Moreover, on some vases we frequently see the two main apotropaic symbols combined in one–a large phallus with an eye or pair of eyes!

This so frequent use of the phallus, may be explained by the absolute supremacy of men (patriarchy) while, in the age of matriarchy, the symbols of fertility were statuettes of women with heavy buttocks and clearly stated the attributes of their sex.

Finally, the last category consists of vases with genuinely erotic representations intended to arouse sexual feeling in the onlooker; we shouldn't though confuse these with pornography as they were intended for use only in the symposia and that explains the fact that most of those vases are *kylikes*.[3]

If we now observe these erotic scenes, we will see that the majority of them picture men with

28. *A marble herm of Hermes from Siphnos. Circa 520 B.C. National Archaeological Museum, Athens, 3728. (Photo: N. A. Vrissimtzis.)*

---

[1] *Sileni:* initially demons of waters and from the 5th cent. B.C. onwards, the inseparable companions of Dionysos. They had a human body, the tail of a horse and were always pictured having an erection. Both Satyrs and Sileni symbolized the primitive forces of nature.

[2] The eye as an apotropaic amulet that protects from the Evil Eye has survived in Greece up to the present day.

[3] *Kylix* (pl. *kylikes*): a sort of shallow wine goblet, with a wide mouth and two handles, used as a drinking cup.

women, few are those with adult men together, even fewer are those with men and male youths, and only one concerns women together but it is not clear if the scene has a truly lesbian character.

All the possible ways and positions of copulation are depicted: vaginal, anal, contact on the thighs, fellatio, cunnilingus, masturbation, use of sex-aids (dildos), *ménage-à-trois* ("threesome"), *soixante-neuf* ("sixty-nine"), sadism, orgies, bestiality, etc.

We should note here that there is differentiation between the erotic representations of the 6th century and those of the 5th and 4th cent. B.C. Up until approximately the end of the 6th century, the scenes depicted, initially on black-figure and later on red-figure[4]

29. *A couple copulating anally. Black-figure vase. Museum of Compiègne.*

vases, include exclusively vaginal and anal intercourse, while scenes of oral sex as well as scenes of orgies are absent. We can therefore speculate that these ways weren't completely acceptable, without of course claiming that they weren't practiced. Besides, art reflects reality only to a certain extent; for example, the figures and the features on the statues were idealized as the Greeks were lovers of beauty and therefore depicted the human body without imperfections.

Scenes of orgies in the same period, concern either Satyrs together or Satyrs and Maenads (women followers of Dionysos), as shown, for example, on a red-figure *lekythos,* now in the Berlin museum. This probably means

---

[4] The two prevailing styles in both the archaic and the classical period. The black-figure vases (7th–6th cent. B.C.), had black figures painted on a red background while the red-figure ones (from the middle of the 6th century onwards), had red figures painted against a black background.

that it was believed that this kind of conduct was not proper for humans. The Greeks believed in Moderation *("Nothing in excess"),* and therefore, every deviance, like unrestrained sexual activity and lust weren't acceptable.

Even masturbation was regarded as something befitting Satyrs rather than humans, and among the latter it was acceptable only for slaves or barbarians.

On a *pelike,* a sort of big amphora, kept in the Villa Giulia in Rome, a wreath-crowned man is shown, with his sandal in his hand about to hit a youth with an erection. The impression conveyed by the scene is that the man is a teacher of some sort and is about to punish the youth who had been caught masturbating.

30. *Courtesan with two dildos. Kylix, circa 500* B.C. *British Museum, E 815.*

Women masturbated also with the help of an artificial penis, the *olisbos* or *baubon.* This forerunner of the modern dildo, was made of soft leather in the wealthy city of Miletus and exported to all countries. Suïdas informs us that the first to use it were of course the women of Miletus, who therefore he characterized as lecherous.

In *Lysistrata,* the heroine of the same name, confesses: "...now the Milesians have rebelled, we can't even get our six-inch Ladies' Comforters which we used to keep as leather rations for when all else failed" (Aristophanes, *Lysistrata* 109). In an fragment of a lost comedy by Herodas *(The Two Friends),* Koritto, a young woman, informs her friend Metro that the best baubons in the city are made by the master-workman Kerdon. Metro then rushes out to get one for herself!

It is not certain whether the olisbos was used in female homosexual relations. It is certain though that it was used by the hetairae at the symposia,

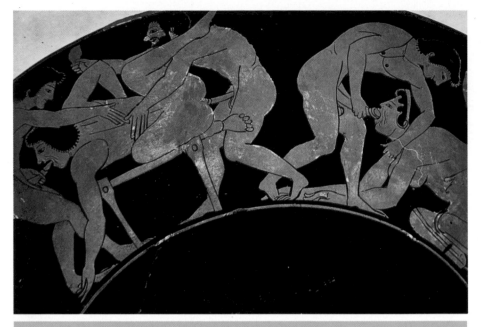

31. An orgy scene by the Pedeius Painter. Red-figure kylix, end of 6th cent. B.C. Courtesy of Musée du Louvre, G 13. (Photo: M. Chuzeville.)

where, with this device, they performed erotic dances for the enjoyment as well as the sexual stimulation of the participants, as shown in relevant illustrations on kylikes. On a kylix by the Nicosthenes Painter, now in the British Museum, a naked hetaira is pictured performing a lascivious dance holding two big artificial penises (Fig. 30).

Later, towards the end of the 6th century, at a time when the symposia had become an established custom, scenes of fellatio, cunnilingus and of orgies begin to appear for the first time on kylikes, the cups used in those drinking-parties. All such illustrations exclusively depict scenes from symposia and this is deduced from the use of various signs and symbols, like flower wreaths on men's heads, flutes and castanets held and played by the hetairae, games such as the *cottabus* (a sort of shooting competition), festive couches, etc. This probably indicates that such conduct was only accepted in the context of the orgiastic intoxication of the symposia.

On one of the most famous of those erotic kylikes, painted by the Pedeius Painter (Fig. 31), we see, among others, a hetaira tilted on a stool, taking a man's penis into her mouth, while at the same time, another man penetrates her from behind. On the same vase, another man, kneeling on a cushion and holding a horn, is offering his penis to another hetaira. Further down, a man is poking his penis into a kneeling hetaira's mouth pushing her head down at the same time. Another man is roaming around with his penis up and holding a big trident, the significance of which escapes us (Fig. 32). A kylix by the Brygos Painter, now in Florence, depicts a man mounting a bent-over hetaira from behind; one of his hands is pushing her head down while the other is holding a sandal over her head which he is about to hit her with. Right next to her, another man with his leg bent towards her head, looks like he is about to kick her. This is one of the very few scenes involving violence.

Another one-of-a-kind illustration is a scene of cunnilingus on a kylix dating from 510 B.C., now in the Berlin museum. Here, among other couples that are entertaining themselves, one stands out, as the man, reclined, is licking the genitals of a hetaira. The fact that this way of sexual contact is nowhere else to be found, implies that it wasn't considered proper for a man; the idea that it was indeed regarded with revulsion can be deduced from excerpts from two Aristophanes' comedies (*Wasps* 1180–183 and *Peace* 884–85).

It is obvious that at a time of complete male supremacy and with the given subjugation of women, a practice such as cunnilingus, where the man offers pleasure to the woman instead of the opposite, was considered im-

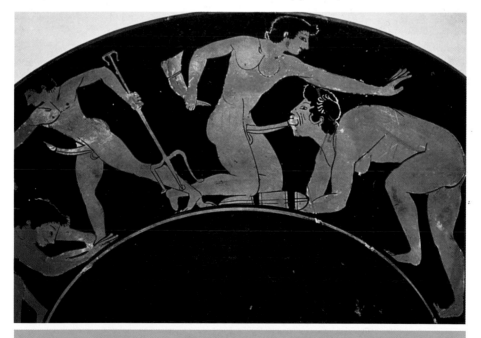

32. Athenian orgy. Red-figure kylix by the Pedeius Painter, end of 6th cent. B.C. Courtesy of Musée du Louvre, G 13. (Photo: M. Chuzeville.)

proper, if not vulgar. This was the case of fellatio as well; even though it is the woman who offers pleasure here, the man remains passive as the woman is the one who acts. But being passive was unacceptable for men, as we will see in the chapter about pederasty. In order to balance this passivity of the man during fellatio, the artists always depict women kneeling, in a position of submission, while their features are altered by the penetration of the penis into their mouth.

A unique scene combining fellatio and cunnilingus in a sixty-nine pose can be seen on a lamp in the museum of Herakleion, Crete, but it is of Roman origin.

It is worth noticing that the classic and most widespread "missionary" position, is nowhere to be seen. On the contrary, we usually see women bent forward (Fig. 33), or kneeling, or lying down on their back with their legs raised onto the man's shoulders; the latter is a rather painful pose for the woman, but has the advantage of offering a clear view of the penis, which was the intention of the artist. The same pose is referred to in Aristophanes' *Lysistrata,* in a way that indicates it was enjoyed by men and commonly practiced. Another pose almost totally absent, is the woman seated on a reclined man; it is rare because the dominant partner here is the female, an idea that was not appreciated by the male clientele.

33. Young prostitute and her customer in the rear-entry pose. Red-figure kylix by the Briseis Painter, circa 480 B.C. Ashmolean Museum–Oxford, 1967.305.

Three reasons explain the unwillingness of the artists to depict these rather traditional positions: first, the woman had to be shown in an submissive way; second, the missionary position is not explicit enough, as the genitals are not visible and therefore was not suitable for a clientele that sought especially this kind of stimulation and third, all erotic scenes are with hetairae, from whom men wanted something more fancy than the ordinary and dull way of copulation they could have anytime with their wives.

In heterosexual relations, it seems that anal penetration was as popular as the vaginal one, and in no text or illustration do we find anything that would condemn it. Thus, it must have been a socially acceptable way of copulation. Despite the fact that on the vases both ways are pictured, we can't decide on which was the most popular or more frequent, as in most illustrations the man is on the back of the woman and the point of penetration of the penis is not clearly visible.

Furthermore, it's not possible for us to know whether women regarded anal coitus (a practice that principally satisfies the man) as acceptable or enjoyable, but it is probable that they preferred it for reasons of contraception.

If we now take a closer look at these erotic scenes, we will observe that sex is practiced solely for pleasure and that

34. A couple making love. Terracotta. Museum of Delos, B 7461. Photo: École Française d'Archéologie, Athènes.

any facial expression that could convey even the most fleeting sentiment is absent. The postures are stiff, and there in no sign of emotional involvement among the participants. This could be due to the fact that couples are very rarely shown in a face-to-face position.

One of the few exceptions is an *oinochoe* ("wine jug") by the Shuvalov Painter, dating from 430 B.C., now in the Berlin museum, that depicts a young man with a hetaira of the same age; he is seated with his penis in erection while the girl, holding him affectionately by his shoulders, is about to settle herself astride his lap. Their heads touch and they are gazing fixedly into each other's eyes; in them, we discern a lot more than mere sexual desire. This illustration is furthermore highly appreciated from an aesthetic point of view–the bodies and the heads form a circle, while the absence of decoration and the plain black background intensify the sense of absorption in each other. It is undoubtedly one of the best examples of Greek erotic painting.

There was no law against bestiality, possibly owing to the fact that it wasn't practiced by the Greeks. The only such scenes are either associated with mythology–like for example the popular myth of Leda and the Swan (Zeus), and others in which Zeus took the form of an animal or bird in order to approach and copulate with beautiful mortal women (Fig. 35)–or concern mythical beings like the Satyrs and the Maenads who are sometimes depicted copulating with animals (Fig. 36).

There was, nonetheless, a law against rape to protect women and children, either free-born or slaves. The penalty was a fine and the offender had to pay it twice over–once to the victim and once to the State. Rape was a serious criminal act and therefore the fine was correspondingly high–according to a law set by Solon, the rapist had to pay a hundred drachmas (Plutarch, *Solon*).

As far as male homosexuality was

35. *Leda and the Swan (Zeus). Mirror from Eretria, 4th cent.* B.C. *National Archaeological Museum, Athens, 7417.*

concerned, that is sexual relations between two adult men, it can be unequivocally stated that it was socially unacceptable and condemned. Various texts, comedies (Aristophanes, *Thesmophoriazusae* 201), and illustrations on vases bear testimony to this.

36. *A graffito drawing of sodomy from the Agora of Athens. Courtesy of "American School of Classical Studies at Athens: Agora Excavations."*

The passive homosexual, not the active one, was the target of social criticism, since he was the one humiliatingly penetrated. Such a thing was inadmissible and disgraceful not from a moral point of view, but simply because the man was mounted and took the role of the woman. This is the reason why no illustrations depicting anal coitus between men have come down to us. Lastly, on a vase dating from circa 470 B.C., right after the end of the Persian wars, a Greek is depicted holding his erect penis and heading for a Persian soldier who has bent forward and assumed an effeminate pose–the scene implies thus the humiliating defeat of the Persians, and how disgraceful it was for a man to be mounted by another.

From the pictorial representations, as well as from the sources, it is clear that neither the Greeks nor the Romans ever practiced circumcision. Moreover, the practice of circumcision by other peoples was jeered at by the former and the latter alike, as shameful and grotesque. The Romans, called the circumcised foreigners *verpus* (circumcised penis) and *recutitus* (skinned).

Let us conclude this chapter by reminding ourselves that vases with erotic scenes were mostly made to order, therefore satisfying the tastes of a specific clientele; in other instances, the artist painted as

37. *A love-making scene on a black-figure kylix. Museum of Compiègne.*

he fancied, always however, with an eye to its commercial value.

The same applies to comedy (a valuable source of evidence): by addressing the middle and the lower class, comedy made use of the appropriate language and of an amount of exaggeration that would serve its purpose of criticizing the upper class.

PROSTITUTION

From such a permissive (at least for men) society, the oldest profession couldn't be absent. We can speculate that prostitution had always been practiced in Greece, under various forms. It is not mentioned by Homer, but this is no reason to believe that it was unknown. Money might have been unknown in the times of Homer, but prostitution is far older than money.

At the beginning of the 6th cent. B.C., the period of uncontrolled prostitution came to an end, when the legislator Solon (639–559 B.C.) established the first brothels in Athens, to help relieve adolescents who had reached the reproductive age and keep them from committing adultery with respectable women. Here is what Athenaeus wrote: "Oh, Solon, you are our benefactor, as our city is full of young men of ardent temperament who could be carried away to punishable acts. But you bought women and installed them in particular places, where they can be at the disposal of all who need them. There they are, naked as nature made them. No surprise. Watch them all! Do you want to be happy? The door will open if you want it to, an *obole* will do...With some coins you can buy a moment of pleasure without risking a single thing. You can pick out the one you prefer–thin, fat, tall, short, young, middle-aged, old–whom you can have in any way. Anybody can enjoy them easily, without any risk, day or night."

It is also said that Solon, with the money raised from the taxation of these first brothels, built a temple dedicated to Aphrodite Pandemos, the patron goddess of hired love, the first temple he built in Attica (Athenaeus 13, 569 d). Thus, the girls of pleasure were, from the 6th cent. B.C. onwards, protected by the State but were also obliged to pay taxes and moreover, were often subjected to market inspection concerning their tariff.

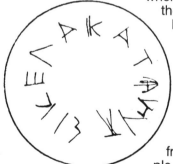

38. *"Sikela* [probably a prostitute] *is lecher*[ous]. Courtesy of the "American School of Classical Studies at Athens: Agora Excavations."

In Greek, the word for whore is *porne,* and derives from the verb *per-nemi* ("to sell"), that is the one who is on sale. From this Greek word, derive the words *porno*-graphy, *porno*grapher, *porno*graphic and *porno*graphically. Initially, the word only

39. *The "Street of the Tombs" in the ancient Athenian cemetery of Kerameikos, adjacent to which were the brothels. (Photo: N. A. Vrissimtzis.)*

described the profession and did not have the derogatory meaning which it acquired later and which it still has today.

The common whore shouldn't be confused with the hetaira of whom we will speak in the next chapter.

As for their origin, the whores were slaves or former slaves that had been freed by a lover or a regular customer who obviously greatly appreciated their merits. They could also be *metoikoi,* that is free but foreign immigrants or even girls that had been abandoned by their parents and ended up in the hands of a procurer.

Finally, they were often the daughters of prostitutes or former prostitutes who learned the secrets of the lucrative profession from their mothers. Occasionally, a free-born Athenian woman could become a prostitute, but this was vary rare and only in the case of extreme poverty.

In Athens, the act of inciting an Athenian woman to prostitution was strictly prohibited and punished by a law set by Solon. As we learn from Plutarch: "[Solon ordered that] if a man gained his end by persuasion he was to be fined twenty drachmas, unless it were with one of those who sell themselves openly...For these go openly to those who offer them their price. Still further, no man is allowed to sell a daughter or a sister, unless he finds out that she is no longer a virgin" (Plutarch, *Solon* xxiii, 1).

The procurers were men or women of the lowest social status who exploited one or more prostitutes, kept in brothels or not. Procuring, if denounced and proved, could even incur the death penalty in the 4th cent.

B.C: [Solon commanded that] "procurers, men or women, be indicted, and if they are convicted, be punished with death" (Aeschines, *Against Timarchus* 184).

Prostitutes fell into various categories, depending on where they frequented and practiced their profession. There were the *chamaitypae,* called so because they worked outdoors, lying down (*chamai typto* = to lie down);

there were the *perepatetikae* ("wanderers") who roamed the streets and aftrer picking up somebody drove him to their houses or to hired rooms or simply in a dark corner; there were the *gephyridae* who gadded about the bridges; others were installed in, or frequented, the public baths, and finally the *katakleistae* ("the shut in") who were kept in brothels.

Another name for brothels was *oikiskoi* ("little houses"), deriving from the word *oikos* ("house"). The same connection is still extant in some languages as for example in Italian– *casino* ("brothel"), from *casa* ("house"). The brothels established by Solon were located in the district of Kerameikos ("the potters' quarter"), on the northwestern outskirts of Athens and next to the graveyard of the same name (Fig. 39).

Little by little, the number of brothels multiplied and as Athenaeus informs us, no city possessed as many whores as Athens did, with the notable exception of Corinth of course, where the famous Temple Prostitution was practiced, as described further down.

During the excavations at Kerameikos, no building was found that could be clearly identified as a brothel; however, other buildings brought to light, such as taverns and inns, could also have been used as brothels, as the numerous findings of objects belonging to women attest to–mirrors, cheap jewelry, jewelry cases, statuettes of Aphrodite, etc. Obviously, brothels also existed in Piraeus, the port-town of Athens, where many ships from faraway places anchored and where there was life and action (Aristophanes, *Peace* 165).

40. *A young man paying a prostitute with a hare. Alabastron, 490 B.C. Museum of Kerameikos, 2713. Deutsches Archäologisches Institut Athen.*

Prostitutes had to pay a special tax to the State, the *pornikon telos* ("prostitute-tax"), collected by a special official. For those kept in a brothel, the tax was paid by their procurer, while those who worked on their own account had to pay it themselves. This prostitute tax must have constituted a considerable income for the State, if we consider the large number of prostitutes. The amount of tax to be paid, was proportional to the prostitute's tariff which was in turn determined by the State, again with the help of an official, the *agoranomos*. A similar tax existed in other Greek cities as well.

The tariff for a visit to a brothel in the 5th cent. B.C., was usually one *obole* (1 drachma = 6 *oboles*), as the historian Athenaeus informs us (13, 568–69), but the girls could also be paid in kind (Fig. 40). There were of course

41. A bronze mirror cover with a scene in a brothel. 4 c. B.C. Museum of Fine Arts, Boston, Res. 08.32c. Gift of E.P. Warren.

cheaper and more expensive prostitutes, while the clients occasionally had to pay extra for special services. For unskilled manual workers, this price corresponded to approximately a day's wages, for skilled workers it was a sixth of their day's wages, while for the well-off citizens, it was very cheap, although the latter scorned the common prostitutes and entertained themselves with the more educated, refined and much more expensive hetairae. Quite a number of illustrations depict scenes in the houses of joy, but the overwhelming majority concerns the admission of the clients, the deal with a woman, the payment and very seldom the sexual act itself. Thus, on various vases, we see young or mature men offering, in advance, a pouch to girls dressed in transparent dresses, the girls embracing the men or sitting on their laps, which meant that they accepted, while some of these scenes are supervised by the owner of the house, usually an elderly former prostitute.

The only perhaps illustrations of copulation in a brothel, and which we can certainly identify with such a place, are on the cover of a mirror from the 4th cent. B.C., kept in the Museum of Fine Arts, Boston (Fig. 41). On the outer and inner part of its cover, two couples are p i c t u r e d, one on each side, making love. What distinguishes the place where the sexual act takes place, are the beds—both are covered with a coverlet and have

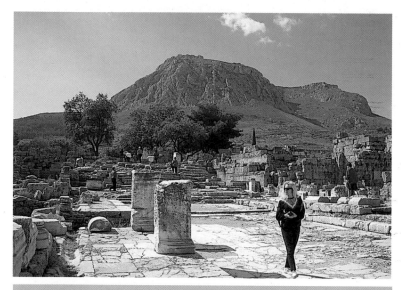

42. *The Acropolis of Corinth on which once stood the temple of Aphrodite, famous for the practice of Temple Prostitution. (Photo: N.A.Vrissimtzis.)*

pillows. The festive couches at the symposia didn't possess either. It is out of the question that the mirror could have belonged to a respectable Athenian woman; judging from its elegance, we suppose that it would have belonged to an expensive prostitute instead.

The subject of Temple Prostitution deserves a special mention. This was a very old institution, found in virtually every community of the Middle East (Phoenicia, Syria, Babylon, Asia Minor) while in the Greek territories it was only recorded in Corinth, and in Paphos and Amathus in Cyprus. The agricultural societies believed in a kind of sympathetic magic, according to which there is mutual influence between similar things. Accordingly, they dedicated some women for life, the *hierodouli,* to the temples of the love-goddess (Ishtar, Astarte, Mylitta, Aphrodite), their duty being to offer themselves for money. Thus, the sexual act performed in honor of the goddess, in accordance with the symbolism and associations referred to in the previous chapter, would induce fertility of women, fertility of the earth and therefore prosperity of the city. Those prostitutes however, were regarded as, and indeed were, temple personnel and consequently the money they collected didn't increase their personal fortune, but was kept in the treasury of the temple.

In Greece, the only place where Temple Prostitution was practiced was the renowned temple of Aphrodite on the Acropolis of Corinth (Fig. 42). Corinth was a very rich city, owing to its strategic position on the isthmus which connected the Peloponnese with continental Greece and, to the fact that it possessed two important harbors–one in the Aegean Sea (Kenchreai) and another in the Ionian Sea (Lechaion). Consequently, a great number of foreigners, mainly sailors and merchants, some quite wealthy, arrived at the city. It was therefore natural for prostitution to flourish. The temple of Aphrodite amassed a thousand courtesans, as Strabo informs us (viii, 378) and accumulated fabulous wealth left by the worshippers and by the customers of the skilled and expensive prostitutes. Hence the well-known maxim: *"Not every man can afford a visit to Corinth"* or as it was latinized by Horace *"Non cuivis homini contingit adire Corithum."*

As the historian Athenaeus relates, when the town was threatened by Xerxes' fleet, the Corinthians asked the prostitutes of the temple to pray; their prayers were heard and when the Persians withdrew defeated, the Corinthians set up in the temple a dedicatory tablet with the names of the prostitutes who with their prayers contributed to the deliverance of the fatherland.

Another far earlier kind of sacred prostitution, which dates back to the matriarchal age, compelled all girls without exception to be deflowered before marriage, giving themselves for money to some stranger, in the temple, for the benefit of the goddess.

THE HETAIRAE

The hetairae were indisputably prostitutes, as they gave themselves for money, but of a higher rank. We could compare them with the Japanese geishas.

The word hetaira means: friend, companion. The hetairae were the men's companions in the symposia and in other social events from which legal wives, sisters and daughters were excluded, owing to the austerity of the morals but also to their own poor education.

The hetairae originated, just as the common whores, in the classes of the slaves, the ex-slaves and the *metoikoi* ("immigrants"). Most of the famous hetairae were metoikoi and came mainly from more developed places, where women undoubtedly enjoyed more freedom, like for example Ionia. Some of them, were either daughters of prostitutes or former prostitutes themselves who had however, managed to ascend professionally, by cultivating their beauty, but also some other skills, as we will see below. Many former prostitutes or hetairae brought up their daughters to be hetairae, hoping that the girls would be someday rich and would take care of them in their old age. Laïs, one of the foremost hetairae of the classical period, was the daughter of the hetaira Timandra, Alcibiades' mistress.

The hetairae owed their widespread reputation mainly to the symposia–drinking-parties, exclusively for men. No tables or chairs were used in the symposia; the participants rested on festive couches and after they had eaten, started drinking wine and talking. Their discussions varied from the commonplace to political and philosophical subjects. They also played games such as the cottabus (a sort of shooting competition) and enjoyed music and dance performed by the hetairae.

At the symposia the hetairae assumed the duties of flute players and dancers, but also of female company in general, as respectable women couldn't assist. When spirits got high and the senses were aroused, the hetairae offered their services to the participants (Fig. 43) and very often, if not always, the symposion wound up in an orgy.

From their duties we can draw the conclusion that they had to have quite a number of qualities and skills: to be polite, to have good manners, to be clean, to play a musical instrument (flute, lyre, tambourine, castanets), to dance and naturally be ready to offer their body without the slightest hesitation.

A widespread impression would have us believe that the hetairae were all highly educated and took part in philosophical discussions, if not teaching philosophy themselves! This was true only for some, very few though, like Leontion, the philosopher Epicurus' companion, Marmarion, Hedia, Erotion and Demelate–all Epicurus' disciples–Aspasia (if she had indeed been originally a hetaira), Hipparchia, the cynic philosopher Crates' companion, and Lamia, who rebuilt the ruined picture-gallery for the Sicyonians (the *Poikile Stoa*). Nevertheless, their principal merits were their exceptional beauty, their wit and their relative competence in discussions.

Not everybody could afford to hire a hetaira. From Atheneaus (xiii, 581), we learn that the notorious Phryne charged a hundred drachmas, while Gnathaena asked once for a thousand drachmas, an extravagance at the time! Phryne, though, was one of the foremost hetairae and the mistress of the sculptor Praxiteles, of the orator Hyperides and of other prominent men who could obviously afford her high price. However, it may well be that the sums mentioned, as well as other sums mentioned for other hetairae, are only the exaggerations of writers who lived and wrote several centuries later.

The fact however remains, that the hetairae were extremely well-paid and as a result they enjoyed a luxurious lifestyle. They lived in big houses, lavishly decorated and even had slaves (although without owning them). Their wealth was exclusively in the form of money, as they couldn't own property. It is mentioned that Phryne, after the destruction of Thebes by the army of Alexander the Great, offered to rebuild the city at her own expense, provided that, at the entrance of the town, an inscription would be placed declaring: *"Alexander destroyed it, Phryne the hetaira rebuilt it"* (Athenaeus xiii, 591d). The truth of this might be questionable, but it is certain that Phryne dedicated a statue of herself decorated with gold, a work by Praxiteles, to the sanctuary of Apollo in Delphi, bearing the inscription: *"Phryne Epicleus Thespike"* (Dedicated by Phryne, the daughter of Epicles, from Thespiai), and had it placed between the statues of the kings Archidamus and Philip (Athenaeus viii, 591 b). Another offering of the same hetaira was a statue of Eros, at the sanctuary of the same name at Thespiai in Boeotia, her hometown.

The hetaira Cottina dedicated the bronze statue of a cow at Sparta, and Athenaeus mentions more, real or imaginary, expensive offerings of other famous hetairae.

By doing so, the hetairae wanted to make their way up in society, in an effort to overcome the traumatic experiences of a deprived childhood and of the inevitable passage from common prostitution. Mere wealth wasn't adequate to serve this purpose, but fame would do. Another way to climb up the social ladder, was to associate their names and occasionally their lives,

43. *Scene at a Symposion. End of 6th century* B.C. *Courtesy of Royal Museums of Art and History–Brussels, R 351.*

with distinguished personalities–statesmen, generals, artists and philosophers.

We know of many such famous couples: Aspasia and Pericles, Phryne and Praxiteles, Timandra and Alcibiades, Leontion and Epicurus, Thaïs and Alexander the Great, Glycera and Menander, Mania and Demetrios Poliorketes, Agathokleia and Ptolemy IV and many others.

The hetairae, especially in the classical era, were favored by the upper class–which they served–due to their physical attributes and not their moral status. It is mentioned that Socrates expressed the wish to meet the famous hetaira Theodote, about whom his disciples often talked. So one day, he finally visited her and admired her beauty, her house and wealth, and when she asked him to visit her more often, he diplomatically replied: "But of course I don't want to be drawn to you: I want you to come to me...and you shall be welcome, unless there's a dearer girl with me!" (Xenophon, *Memorabilia* iii, xi).

The word is that, on one occasion in his youth, the renowned politician Themistocles put four hetairae on his chariot and rode around the city in the rush hour, in order for everybody to see him (Athenaeus). Alcibiades openly wandered about always accompanied by a hetaira, until he finally got involved with Timandra.

When defending his mistress Phryne, brought before the court for impiety, the orator Hyperides did not hesitate to tear her clothes off and lay bare the beauty of her body; the judges, having admired her truly magnificent figure, acquitted her. We should note here that Phryne's real name was Mnesarete ("the one who considers Virtue"), an inappropriate name for a woman who was selling her body! Phryne, was a nickname given to her because her complexion was yellowish (*phrynos* in Greek describes a yellowish frog). Despite this, she was much sought-after, as for the Greeks, a beautiful body was appreciated more than a pretty face or the colour of skin. Owing to this perfect body of hers, Praxiteles used her as model for his statues of Aphrodite.

The hetairae, being women and indeed not Athenians, still needed a protector (not necessarily a procurer), who would look after them in case they found themselves involved in scandals and trouble (law-suits, etc.).

Lastly, the dream of every hetaira, even of the most famous one, was to find a wealthy citizen who would take her into his house as his concubine, where she could live comfortably in a relationship similar to marriage and have children. That was the case of the hetaira Neaera, who after several adventures, ended up living with Stephanos, an Athenian citizen, having illegally appropriated the status of a legal wife,

something that resulted in the well-known trial. It is also said that Themistocles' mother, a certain Abrotonon from Thrace, was a former hetaira, and so was the mother of the Athenian general Timotheus, a fact that didn't hinder the ascension of either men to the highest offices. Demosthenes, according to Athenaeus (xiii, 592 e), was inclined to sensual pleasures and was living with a hetaira, from which he had children. Aristotle himself, when widowed, lived with the hetaira Herpyllis who gave him a son, Nicomachus, and for whom he wrote the *Nicomachaean Ethics* (Athenaeus xiii, 589 c).

On the other hand, the Old Comedy

44. *Young hetaira prepares to take a bath. 480 B.C. Courtesy of Royal Museums of Art and History–Brussels, A 889.*

denounced the hetairae as liars and misers, who were greedy, cunning and degenerate, as many writers of the time also did. Let's not forget the virtual war declared against Aspasia, Pericles' companion, from the same circles (comic poets, writers, etc.).

An immigrant, born in Miletus of Ionia, Aspasia settled in Athens in 450 B.C. Her background remains unclear. She was a beautiful, intelligent, educated and perceptive woman. Socrates, especially appreciated her oratorical skill (Plato, *Menexenus*). Aeschines, the philosopher, wrote for her the work *Aspasia* and Plutarch held her in high esteem, although he was not her contemporary.

On the contrary, however, the comic poets portrayed her as a concubine (Cratinus 241), as a hetaira or prostitute (Eupolis 98), even as a common procurer who maintained a brothel! (Aristophanes, *Acharnians* 524, and Athenaeus xiii, 569). It is obvious of course, that it was the task of the comedy to ridicule, and titillating subjects as that, attracted the public. Furthermore, much of the criticism against her was actually addressed to Pericles himself.

From the period of the New Comedy onwards, the hetairae were treated with tolerance, if not at times favorably. A case in point is Menander's comedy of situations *The Arbitrants,* where the hetaira Abrotonon, a kind-hearted girl, helps her lover Charisios find his lost child.

PEDERASTY

We have to clarify from the start that pederasty did not have a homosexual character, and therefore it should not be confused with pedophilia–the sexual abuse of children. The word pederasty denotes the spiritual affection and admiration for a boy, and in ancient Greece was not used obscenely. The fact that today in some languages the word has an derogatory sexual association is due to misinterpretation as we will see below.

It is well known that from the post-matriarchal age onwards, male homosexuality started to flourish in all those societies, ancient or modern, where women were (or still are) socially and sexually restrained. This occurred among virtually all ancient peoples, but especially among nomadic ones and mostly during periods of migration, war and so on, when women were either absent or outnumbered by men.

In the more military-oriented societies, for example in Sparta, Thebes or Crete, boys left their families from a very young age (in Sparta from the age of seven) and lived in military communes together with their peers as well as with older men, learning the life of a soldier. It is there, and also in the palaestrae and the gymnasia, where they trained naked, that pederasty developed. In so saying, we mean that whereas homosexuality had always existed, pederasty is a phenomenon that appeared approximately in the middle of the 6th century and flourished until roughly the end of the 4th cent. B.C. The possibility of it being older is not ruled out, but there are no relevant references in the sources.

In Homer, there is no testimony and indeed not even a hint of such a thing and it is certain that if pederasty had existed, he would have mentioned it in some way. We should also note that the close relationship between Achilles and Patroclus is described in the *Iliad* only as a pure friendship. It was Aeschylus, much later (5th cent. B.C.) who, in his tragedy *Myrmidons* gave the first homosexual connotation to it. Furthermore, nothing to prove that pederasty had existed earlier is found in the art of the archaic period. Besides, the Greek writers them-

45. *Marble statue of Aphrodite grooming her hair after a bath. Courtesy of the Museum of Rhodes. 5693.*

selves, admit that such a thing didn't exist in remote times, when ethics hadn't evolved enough for something like that (Lucian, *Amores* 35). As Plutarch says, pederasty appeared when youths started training in the palaestrae and the gymnasia (Plutarch, *Erotikos* 751).

In the classical era, when philosophy, poetry, music and athletics were constantly developing, men become more and more refined, both physically and mentally, while women remained excluded from all the above. The result was that men had nothing to discuss with their wives who, being always restricted within the house, had developed a simplicity of character and a mental narrowness. Thus, the Greeks, who had always been lovers of beauty, had no choice but to turn to the beauty and harmony of the well-trained male body and to the cultured male spirit. Those two went together as the maxim attests to: *"Sound in body, sound in mind."* This also explains the fact that in the archaic and classical periods we almost exclusively find male naked statues. Female naked bodies, on the contrary, are represented in sculpture only towards the end of the 4th cent. B.C., with the first statues of goddess Aphrodite (Fig. 45).

The body was thus trained in the palaestrae and the mind in the schools. But the latter only appeared in the middle of the 4th cent. B.C. Where were the young citizens instructed earlier? The schools could only offer rudimentary knowledge, like reading and writing, arithmetic and music, while philosophy was taught only in special philosophy schools. Who would then teach the young Athenian the secrets of social life, the functions of the State, virtue, ethos, but also the pitfalls and dangers of life? How would a youth on his own and without help, make acquaintances and friendships that would be useful and supportive later in his life?

Therefore, he needed someone apart from his trainer and teacher. His father certainly couldn't be the one, since he was always out of the house, busy working or participating in public affairs. His mother, moreover, uneducated as she obviously was, couldn't help in this matter. Besides, family in those times lacked the cohesion and function it acquired a lot later; it was instead a quite loose and brittle connection and therefore couldn't assume an instructional role.

Here pederasty enters the picture: an educated adult was charged with transmitting his knowledge and experience to an adolescent, and with helping him become a responsible citizen. The adult in return, admired and enjoyed the beauty, strength and vigor of the youth. A two-way communication was thus created for the benefit of both.

The concept that strength, courage, knowledge and virtue can pass down from the older and more experienced to the younger and inexperienced, but also that the vigor of the young can be conveyed to the older through a close relationship, is primordial. Cannibalism in primitive societies rests on the same principle.

It is thus clear, that pederasty was an institution of noble and high ideals. For this same reason it shouldn't be identified with homosexuality. And that's what differentiates it from any similar institution found in any other civilization.

Pederasty followed concrete sets of rules. In this relationship, the adult was called *erastes* ("lover") and the minor *eromenos* ("the beloved"). The beloved had to be between twelve and eighteen years old. Any relationship with a child younger or older than this, was inconceivable, as it was at the age of twelve that children entered puberty, a period when they started forming a personality and when they precisely needed an instructor. On the other hand, the continuation of this relationship after the age of 18, was considered unacceptable and faced general disapproval.

The erastes had to be from the age of twenty up, which means that he had passed through the stage of the eromenos and had adequate social experience and education to convey to his own eromenos in turn.

Acquaintances were made in the gymnasia and the palaestrae, where young men trained under the supervision of the *paedotribes* ("coach"). There, adult men could watch youths training naked, admire their harmonious bodies, but also their abilities and their performances. The aspiring erastes approached the boy that was the object of his admiration and tried to gain his favor with various presents, as we see on vases of the period. These presents had a symbolic or instructional character. Symbolic presents were the flower wreath, the symbol of value and virtue, and the cockerel, which symbolized virility and power. The cockerel, though, used in cock-fights, also taught the youth the fighting spirit and aggressiveness, elements that were necessary for molding the aspiring young citizen's martial virtue. Another animal with instructional significance was the hare (Fig. 46). The youth would set the hare free and a dog behind to chase it, learning the joy and pleasure of hunting this way.

Other animals offered as presents were deer and birds, but also dogs and wildcats. Instructional presents were the lyre, the flute, writing boards and oil flasks for the anointment of the body. Lastly, a present that was also proof of admiration was a vase, with the boy's name written on it, followed by the word *kalos* ("beautiful"). Many such vases have come down to us,

46. *A man offering a hare to a youth. National Archaeological Museum, Athens, 1413. (Photo: N. A. Vrissimtzis.)*

all dating from the period during which pederasty appeared and flourished (Fig. 47).

The erastes ordered such a vase with the name of his beloved boy on it. However, there was also an industry specializing in vases with the inscription *o pais kalos* ("the boy is beautiful") which were suitable for any occasion, and vases bearing the names of the most beautiful youths of Athens, for which there would certainly be demand on the part of their aspiring lovers.

The erastes expressed his admiration and preference with presents, whereas the eromenos, according to the unwritten rules of pederasty, shouldn't express himself, but nurture only a friendly affection and esteem for the erastes. Thus, the attraction was in fact one-sided as the boy didn't participate, least of all sexually as we will see below.

The relationship was, by principle, based on inequality, that is between an educated adult and a crude young boy. This explains the fact that their relationship couldn't continue after the eromenos had reached manhood, at the age of 18, as the element of inequality and consequently the instructional purpose disappeared. On occasions where it continued, it would probably become a homosexual relationship between two adults, something that was socially unacceptable.

As long as the relationship lasted, the erastes taught the eromenos ways of behavior, rules of politeness, moral values, discipline, but also the basics about social life, legislation and foreign affairs of the city; moreover, he initiated him into the world of Art and Theater, things not taught in school, but which were indispensable if the youth was to become a citizen with conviction, judgment, ethos and virtue.

So far, it is obvious that pederasty was based on high principles, while the

47. *"Alkaios seems kalos [beautiful] to Melis." Courtesy of "American School of Classical Studies at Athens: Agora Excavations."*

48. *Men and youths flirting. The second couple from left is engaged sexually. Black-figure amphora by the Painter of Berlin, circa 540 B.C. British Museum, 1865.11.*

sexual part of the relationship remained subordinate and included only some discreet expressions of passion on the part of the erastes.

As far as this aspect of the relationship is concerned, the sources almost neglect to mention it, but there is pictorial evidence, on various vases. Often enough, we see adults touching the genitals of youths, but never the opposite. The sexual act itself was performed (if and when so) exclusively between the youths' thighs, in a face-to-face position (Fig. 48). All the relative scenes agree on that. There are none showing anal penetration; illustrations depicting or implying it have nothing to do with pederasty; they refer either to mythical creatures (Satyrs, Sileni), or show scenes from symposia involving male prostitution, or finally, depict a homosexual act between adults.

The act between the thighs of the eromenos, was the only permitted one according to the unwritten rules of pederasty, but also according to the social and moral codes. The reasons for this are simple and easily understandable. Anal penetration would reduce the aspiring young citizen to the woman's place, to the position of sexual object. According to the prevailing principles of the era, the penetration by the penis whether of the vagina, anus or the mouth, was an aggressive act implying power–an act proper only for men; while on the other hand, it signified the submission of the penetrated person. Submission and passivity however befitted only women and slaves.

It was thus inconceivable for a future Athenian citizen to be put through such humiliation, reducing himself to the woman's role. It wasn't a matter of morality, but one of social honor. Only with women and slaves could one communicate sexually this way.

Among the worst curses for a man were the words *katapygon* (lecher, degenerate, lewd), (Fig. 49), and *evryproktos* or *lakoproktos* ("broad-bummed").

In no case was anal penetration permitted to boys who would later become responsible citizens, take up offices and administrate the fortunes of the State, as such a thing would reduce them to the disgraceful role of the object, which was incongruous to the role they would then be called upon to play in society. Consequently, contact on the thighs safeguarded the eromenos' dignity and honor.

Another important element was the boy's non-participation, which, combined with the inviolability of his anus, differentiated his position from the passive female companion's role. All the surviving vases agree on that. Whereas the erastes has an erection or is performing the act on the eromenos' thighs, the latter's penis is always shown flaccid (Fig. 50). Furthermore, the expression on the boys' faces is always distant and indifferent while the erastes' faces reflect passion. If a youth enjoyed this kind of sexual act, he was considered a male prostitute and faced general disapproval.

Even though there were rare instances of sexual abuse, this in no way discredits the institution of pederasty, nor its ethos. Chronologically, pederasty is limited to between the 6th and the 4th cent. B.C. and found only among members of the upper class. Besides, it couldn't be otherwise, as the role of pederasty was educational and therefore the lower classes of peasants, manual workers, *metoikoi* and slaves were excluded for lack of the required cultural and moral status.

49.

"Titas the Olympic victor is a lecherous fellow"

The inscription is written around the rim of a coarse household water jar, which may have been presented to Titas as a parody of the splendid Panathenaic amphorae that were given as prizes in games. The Olympic victory is presumably figurative, to suggest Titas' championship status in his other capacity.

Courtesy of "American School of Classical Studies at Athens: Agora Excavations."

The metoikoi and the slaves in particular, didn't even possess political rights and consequently lacked the civil conviction required for the instructional purpose of pederasty (Aeschines, *Against Timarchus* 57). The ancient texts that deal with the subject refer always to noble and wealthy citizens.

Furthermore, pederasty required time and money. The aspiring erastes had to spend quite a long time in the palaestrae and the gymnasia where youths trained, which meant that he must have been fi-

50. *A man titillating a boy. Red-figure kylix by the Brygos Painter, circa 480 B.C. Ashmolean Museum–Oxford, 1967.304.*

nancially secure and have had plenty of free time. He also had to spend a fairly large amount of money on presents in order to win the boy's favor, but also to keep it, as he faced competition from others.

Pederasty was therefore time-consuming and costly, thus excluding the lower classes.

The fact that pederasty would sometimes involve sexual acts is undeniable, but this doesn't mean that sexual abuse of youths was legal or it was tolerated by the State. On the contrary, it was illegal and incurred severe punishment. Testimony to this are such laws as this one: "If any Athenian shall have given himself as a passive homosexual he shall not be permitted to become one of the nine Archons, nor to assume the office of priest, nor shall he act as an advocate for the State, nor shall he ever hold any office whatsoever, either at home or abroad, whether filled by lot or by election, nor shall he be sent as a herald; he shall not take part in a debate, nor be present at the public sacrifices; when the citizens are wearing garlands, he shall wear none; and he shall not enter within the limits of the place that has been purified for the assembling of the people. If any man who has been convicted of prostitution act contrary to these prohibitions, he shall be put to death" (Aeschines, *Against Timarchus* 19).

To prove how strict the law was, and whether it was enforced or not, we will mention the case of Timarchus, in the speech against whom, Aeschines invoked the above law. Timarchus was a respectable citizen, a politically active public figure, accused by his political opponents of supposed prostitution. Two of his ex-lovers claimed that as a youth, he wasted their fortunes, but also those of others, in prodigalities. These testimonies alone weren't adequate to prove the perpetration of the offense of prostitution, but somehow the jury was convinced and Timarchus was sentenced to deprivation of his political rights, on the grounds that "the man who has made traffic of the shame of his own body, he would be ready to sell the common interests of the city also" (Ibid. 29).

The disgrace was so enormous that Timarchus in shame took his own life!

Aeschines mentions another law that prevented the aspiring erastes from meeting and frequenting with boys: "The teachers of the boys shall not open the schools before sunrise and shall close them before sunset. No adult shall be allowed in, unless he be a son of the teacher, a brother, or a brother-in-law. If one, despite this interdiction, enters the school, he shall be punished with death. Also, those in charge of the gymnasia shall under no conditions allow any adult to sit with the children in the festivities of Hermes. If he allows this and does not drive them away, he will be found guilty of violating the law concerning corruption of free-born children" (Ibid. 12).

And further down another law by Solon: "If any Athenian shall outrage a free-born child he should be denounced to the legislators by his father, who should also state the penalty he thinks appropriate. If the court condemn the accused to death, he shall be delivered to the constables and be put to death the same day...." (Ibid. 16).

Another of Solon's laws is mentioned by Demosthenes: "If anyone assaults any child, or woman or man–whether free or slave–or commits an offense against the above, should be denounced to the legislators by any Athenian who desires and who has the right to do so,. The judges shall bring the case within thirty days from the day of the indictment before the Iliaia [court instituted by Solon and which later became the supreme court of Athens], provided public affairs allow it; otherwise, the trial should be carried out as soon as possible. After the trial and provided he is found guilty, he should immediately be sentenced to imprisonment or fined" (Demosthenes, *Against Medeion* 47).

Demosthenes also mentions that Solon "...absolutely forbade such men [homosexuals] to take any share in the counsels of the State" (Demosthenes, *Against Androtion* 30).

In Sparta now, according to a law set by Lycurgus, pederasty was strictly forbidden: "If one appeared who desired children's bodies, this Lycurgus considered to be obscene and instituted that men should abstain from them, just as parents abstain from their own children and brothers from their brothers" (Xenophon, *De Republica Lacedaemoniorum* ii, 13).

Plutarch adds to that: "If one is accused of approaching [children] with bad intentions, he should be considered dishonorable for the rest of his life" (*Instituta Laconica* 7, 237 c).

About Sparta, we have yet another testimony from Aelian: "Spartan love had nothing to do with obscenities. If ever a youth dared to accept abuse against him, or if another youth tried to sexually abuse another, it was in no one's interest to disgrace Sparta thus. In such a case they were either exiled, or even worst, put to death" (Aelian, *Various History* iii, 10).

About Sparta again, Maximus of Tyre writes: "Spartan men do fall in love with Spartan boys, but only as someone falls in love with a beautiful statue" (xxvi, 8).

Herodotus, Thucydides, Plutarch, Diodorus Sikulus and others also bear testimony to the penalization of the sexual abuse of children.

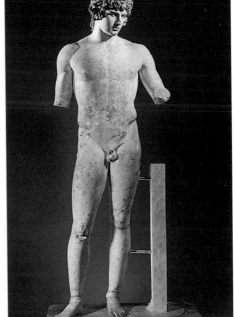

51. Marble statue of Antinous, the beloved friend of the emperor Hadrian, A.D. 138, Museum of Delphi, 1718.

To conclude this chapter we must underline that the noble institution of pederasty should not be confused with pedophilia, and that homosexuality in ancient Greece was simply tolerated and by no means widespread, nor did it constitute a norm of the Greek culture! The occasional sexual incidents of pederasty, on the other hand, were strictly punished by the law.

Therefore, any attempt to present homosexuality and pedophilia as something natural, widespread and admissible in ancient Greek society, falls apart before evidence of such strict legislation, which proves the Greeks' aversion to abnormal relations.

As regards the supposedly homosexual relationship between Zeus and Ganymedes (Fig. 52), from which homosexuals claim their origin, Xenophon writes: "And I aver that in the case of Ganymede, it was not his person but his spiritual character that influenced Zeus to carry him up to Olympus. This is confirmed by his name...[it] signifies not physically but mentally attractive; hence his honor among the gods" (Xenophon, *Symposion* viii, 30).

Different opinions on homosexuality and pederasty, expressed by certain writers trying to picture ancient Greece as the paradise of homosexuality, and the Greeks as having a natural inclination towards one's own sex, is nothing but mere wishful thinking on their part.

52. *Zeus and Ganymedes. Terra-cotta statue, 470 B.C. Museum of Olympia, T 2.*

FEMALE HOMOSEXUALITY

We don't know much about female homosexuality in ancient Greece as, firstly, in a male-dominated society male writers were very little interested in purely feminine issues and secondly, female homosexual love was obviously less widespread than male, as it is in modern times. References to it are scarce but nonetheless disapproving.

The dictionary of Suïdas, refers to the women of Miletus as *"tribads* and wrongdoers" because they made love between themselves and indeed used the *olisbos* ("dildo"), an artificial penis made of soft leather. The word *tribad* ("she who rubs") means lesbian and derives from the verb *trivo* ("to rub") for obvious reasons. Other words to denote the same thing were *hetairistria* and *dihetairistria,* both deriving from *hetaira.* In Latin, the respective term is *frictrix* from the verb *fricare* "to rub".

The term that has prevailed in almost every language though, is the Greek word *lesvia* ("lesbian"), derived from the Greek island of Lesbos, the home of Sappho (Fig. 53), who is wrongly thought of as the major priestess of female homosexual love.

In the dialogue "Klonarion and

53. *Portrait of Sappho. Mosaic, 3rd century A.D. Museum of Sparta, 9. (Photo: N. A. Vrissimtzis.)*

54. *Statue of a Hermaphrodite, a mythical creature of double sexual nature. Post-Hellenistic period. Museum of Dion, 3.*

Leaina" from Lucian's *Dialogues of Courtesans* there is an explicit description of a scene with lesbians. Leaina, a guitar-player, tells her friend Klonarion what happened to her in the house of Megilla, a rich hetaira from Lesbos:

"[she, and Demonassa the Corinthian] *asked me to play the guitar and after a while, they got drunk and Megilla said to me:*

"Time for bed, Leaina, and since it's late, stay here and sleep with us. We'll put you in the middle." ...At the beginning they kissed me like men, not only on the lips but inside the mouth too, and rubbed my breasts and Demonassa even bit me between her kisses...After a while, Megilla, blushing, pulled off a wig she was wearing–which didn't show at all–and appeared close-cropped, like a robust athlete. I got scared, but she said: "Have you seen, Leaina, such a beautiful boy before?"

"But, Megilla, I don't see one here," I said. "Don't call me Megilla," she replied, "I'm Megillos and I have married Demonassa who is my wife."... "So, Megillos, you are a man and you've been concealing it?...Do you have though, what men have, to do to Demonassa what men do?" "No, Leaina, I don't have it, and neither do I need it. I can do my job in a much better way, as you'll find out." "Are you a hermaphrodite then* (Fig. 54), *one of those who have both?", I asked..."No, Leaina," she replied, "I was born like any other woman. But my character and desires are mannish... Just come closer and you'll see." And I let her, dear Klonarion... But don't ask me to tell you more as it is so obscene that, by Aphrodite, I can't go on..." (Dialogues of Courtesans 5).* Plutarch mentions that in Sparta, even honest married women fell in love with young girls, without though clarifying whether it was sexual or spiritual love. No other personality has ever been so closely associated with female homosexuality as the famous poetess Sappho, or Psappha, as her name would sound in the local Aeolic dialect.

Sappho was born around 612 B.C. on the island of Lesbos, perhaps in the city of Eressos or maybe in Mitylene.

Called by many the "tenth Muse" (*Anthology Palatinus* ix, 506, etc.), she was, together with her compatriot poet Alcaeus, the leading poet of the 6th cent. B.C. Socrates, in Plato's *Phaedrus* (235), calls her "Sappho the beautiful," while Alcaeus describes her as "dark-haired, kind-hearted and sweet."

Morals and customs in the Aeolic cities, of which Lesbos was one, differed from those of continental Greece and women enjoyed a certain freedom they had preserved from the times of Homer and they could even be educated in special schools for girls. Let us remember here, that in comparison, not even in the golden era of Pericles were there such schools in Athens.

Sappho's father was called Scamandronymus and her mother Cleïs. She had three brothers: Charaxus, who spent quite a long time in the Greek colony Naucratis in Egypt, and was married to the hetaira Rhodope; the handsome Larichus who was appointed cupbearer in the Town Hall of Mitylene and lastly Eurygius about whom we know nothing but his name. Sappho married a certain Cercylas from the island of Andros *(Suïdas)* and according to the tradition had a daughter by him, Cleïs, named after her mother. Sappho got involved in public affairs and was exiled for sometime to Italy by the tyrant Pittakus.

She kept a school for young girls, a sort of boarding school where they were taught poetry, music, singing and dance. Apparently, these didn't serve as qualifications for future employment, but just as general knowledge and for the development of the personality. Life in that school, the "house of the Muses" as Sappho called it (*Fragment* 136), was communal and every time a new girl came, or an old one left to marry, a celebration was given and Sappho wrote a poem for the occasion.

The names of her favorite students have come down to us, either in the fragments of her own poetry or mentioned later by Maximus of Tyre: Gyrina, Atthis, Anactoria, Gongyla, Arignota, Mnasidica, Euneica, Telesippa, Nossis, Megara, Anagora, Gorgo, Eranna, Cleïs. It is said that the last one was her daughter, as in a poem Sappho refers to her as follows: "I have a daughter fair Cleïs, and none so loved as she, not all the Lydian land, nor Lesbos lovely strand can weigh her worth to me." Yet, it is possible that the poem only refers to a beloved student of hers and that "daughter" is just a poetic expression and manifestation of love, as it is indisputable that she felt love, affection and devotion for her girls.

One of her most beloved girls was Atthis:

Our Atthis then afar is sped,
And I in sooth would fain be dead.
She, as she went, was weeping still,

And thus said sobbing in my ear,
"How sad our lot, O Sappho dear;
Ah, but I go against my will!"

And her I answered thus again:
"Good luck go with thee, but remain
Mindful of me, whose only care

Thou wast; or else, if thou forget
I may not, but remind thee yet
How sweet a life was ours, how fair!"

And again on Atthis:

Love's palsy yet again my limbs doth wring
That bitter-sweet resistless creeping thing.
At this, all thought of me thou now dost hate,
And hoverest ever at Andromeda's gate.

Another beloved girl was Gongyla:

I bid thee hither come, and God thee bless
Sweet Gongyla; put on thy milky-white dress.
Oh God what desire in your beauty lies.

Other beloved students were Mnasidica and Gyrinna:

Though delicately-soft Gyrinna be
Yet Mnasidika more fair than she

It is, however, open to doubt as to whether these relations were of a sexual or platonic nature, much as Socrates' relations with his students were.
Sappho wrote mostly monodies (to be sung accompanied by the lyre), but also *epithalamia* (wedding-songs) as well as epigrams and iambs. From these, only one complete ode and many fragments from others survive. The intense feeling and the sensual atmosphere of her work nurtured the myth about her personal life and the close relations she might have had with her students. She wrote about separation, loneliness, old age and mostly, love.
This great teacher and poetess (Fig. 55), considered equal to Homer, had a tragic end: she took her own life on the island of Leucas jumping off a cliff as her love for a certain Phaon was spurned. The geographer Strabo writes: "Leucas has a temple dedicated to Apollo Leucatas, and the Leap, which, it was thought, was a termination of love. Here Sappho first it is said

(according to Menander) in pursuit of the haughty Phaon, and urged by maddening desire, threw herself from the aerial rock" (x, 452); an act which casts serious doubt on her alleged exclusive interest in women.

The arguments for her hypothetical inclination towards women rely on certain passages of her poetry, which is far too fragmentary to tell the full story. Surely not hard evidence!

On the contrary, not only was she once married and most probably had a daughter, but also she took her own life for an unhappy love affair with a man.

We believe therefore that her case has been misunderstood, if not twisted on purpose, by ancient and modern writers, and that she was no more a lesbian than Galileo Galilei was a charlatan.

It is noteworthy that there are no representations on vases depicting women making love together. This perhaps indicates that neither artists nor customers were interested in such subjects.

55. *Sappho (detail). Courtesy of Staatliche Antikensammlungen und Glyptothek, Munich. SH 2416.*

In ancient times, female homosexuality did not find corresponding literary or artistic expression.

GLOSSARY

Aghape: in Greek, love (the Christian concept).

Agora: the main square of a town, the marketplace.

Agoranomos: official inspecting the prices of goods and services offered.

Andron: the special place of a house where men slept.

Apokalypteria: the rite of the unveiling of the bride.

Apotropaic: an amulet to ward off evil.

Archon: one of nine elected officials who governed ancient Athens.

Cottabus: a sort of shooting competition at the symposia.

Demos: a small self-governed territory and its inhabitants.

Edna: in Homeric times, gifts given by the groom-to-be to his future father-in-law.

Ekdosis: the handing over of the bride to her future husband's family.

Engyesis: in the post-Homeric period, a sort of an unwritten wedding contract.

Epigamy: the right (granted to foreigners) to marry Athenians.

Epikleros: a woman who inherits from her father.

Epinetron: a device used by women during the processing of wool.

Epithalamion: a special wedding-song, sung the first night of the wedding.

Erastes: in pederasty, the adult who loves and instructs a young boy.

Eromenos: in pederasty, a youth who is loved and instructed by an adult.

Eros: an intense feeling of attraction to someone or something. Also, a Greek god.

Fratria: the union of several families of the same lineage, to protect the common interests.

Gamelion: the 7th month of the Attic calendar, corresponding to January–February.

Gymnasion: a special place for athletic training.

Gynaekonitis: a special section of the house where women dwelt.

Herms: marble pillars with a head of Hermes and a phallus.

Hetairae: courtesans of the highest rank.

Hierodouli: prostitutes working in the temples of Aphrodite.

Holy Matrimony: a rural ritual related to the fertility of the earth.

Hymenaeus: the wedding-song, sung during the nuptial procession.

Kalos: beautiful. It was written on vases preceded by the name of a youth.

Katapygon: lecherous, lewd, degenerate. The worst curse for a man!

Kylix: a shallow wine goblet with a large mouth and two handles.

Loutrophoria: a procession to bring water for the bride's purification bath.

Loutrophoros: a special vase used as above.

Metoikos: an immigrant, not having civil or political rights.

Nymphagogeia: the wedding procession to the bride's new home.

Nympheftria: the bridesmaid, usually the bride's best friend.

Oikos: house in its broader sense, meaning: domicile, family, property.

Oinochoe: a medium size vase used to serve wine.

Olisbos (or *baubon*): an artificial penis made of soft leather, the forerunner of dildo.

Paedotribes: coach. A man responsible for the physical education of young boys.

Pais amphithales: a boy who served bread to the guests at the wedding.

Palaestra: a special place where the athletes would train in boxing and wrestling.

Parochos: the bridegroom's best man.

Pederasty: an institution according to which an educated adult was charged with the social education of a youth.

Philo: in ancient Greek, to love.

Philotis: in ancient Greek, love.

Polis: in the ancient meaning of the word, a group of citizens, a city-state.

Porne: the common whore.

Prochous: a medium size vase having one handle, a long neck and a narrow mouth.

Proika: dowry. No wedding could be concluded without it.

Symposion: drinking-parties exclusively for men.

Talanton: monetary unit equal to 6,000 Attic drachmas. Also, unit of mass equal to 26 kg.

Temple Prostitution: a very old institution according to which prostitutes gave themselves for money in the temple of Aphrodite, for the benefit of the goddess.

Tribas: in ancient Greek, lesbian.